"Jia. She is our very own real-life Wonder Woman. *The Tell* is her backstory. Who she is now was chiseled from the heart-breaking, gut-wrenching environment she was born into. Jia was created to survive her many battles and then teach through her art, stories, and paintings that to fight, we will emerge wounded, yet those wounds become our warrior marks, and we, too, become a Wonder."

—KRISTI MOYA, FILMMAKER, SCREENWRITER, AND COUNCIL MEMBER OF THE CHIRICAHUA APACHE NATION

"Jia Apple gives us a mosaic novel, *The Tell*, comprising 365 days taken from across a life to read as a single day. Apple's voice rises as one of the Plains' great voices along the likes of Willa Cather and Allison Russell. She restlessly voices the changing moods and broken seasons of fear, frustration, and doubt and sees them ripen into creativity, wonder, and joy. A monumental achievement."

—JAMES DURHAM, AUTHOR OF *THE DARK WINDOW* AND *THE DELTA QUEEN*

"I loved this wonderfully touching memoir about the life, growth, and evolving perspective of Jubilee Given. It is a potent narrative, conveying the balancing act of a person constantly striving to do their best and find their way to love and self-acceptance. Despite wading through thickets of difficulty and deluges of abuse, Jubilee's harrowing path leads her to find love and joy in life and, subsequently, to the joyful rewards that can be found in family and community. Most importantly, Jubilee finds herself. Her happiness with what she discovers made me feel there is hope for all of us to do the same."

—ALAN ALLINGER, AUTHOR OF *FOUND LEANING AGAINST THE SECOND DOORWAY* AND *CAPTURED WITHIN WAKING MOMENTS*

"*The Tell* stopped my heart. Written from the depths of Jia Apple's soul, it escorts us through fear and trauma into hope and possibility. Artist, singer, and storyteller Jia takes the reader with her on a life-changing creative journey. This is a work for the ages."

—BARBARA A. BENNETT, PH.D., FOUNDER OF STYLE AND SUBSTANCE EDITORIAL SERVICES AND PUBLISHING CONSULTANTS

THE
Tell

THE
Tell

A DAY IN THE LIFE OF JUBILEE GIVEN

JIA APPLE

AWAKEN VILLAGE
PRESS

Printed in the United States of America.

Editing by: Barbara Bennett, Ph.D.
Ponder Goddard, Ph.D.
Cover and interior design by: Andrea Gibb
Author photo by: Barb Chandler

To contact the author or for permission requests, email:
jia@thepictureseer.com.

ISBN 978-1-957408-06-4 (paperback)
ISBN 978-1-957408-07-1 (ebook)
ISBN 978-1-7356582-9-2 (hardcover)

Library of Congress Control Number: 2024914442

Published by Awaken Village Press
Sioux Falls, South Dakota, U.S.A.
www.awakenvillagepress.com

AUTHOR'S NOTE

The names and places in this book have been changed; however, the events in these pages are true to the best of my recollection. I have taken some artistic license around early childhood memories while staying true to the mood, personalities, and general course of events as Jubilee (as myself) experienced them. I also projected a few future events because, even though I don't have that knowledge, I thought it would be fun to play with the future life of Jubilee Given. I even guessed the day I may die, but who knows.

I sometimes say to God that my life should have come with a content warning, so in the spirit of good faith, I say to you: gird your loins. Overall, my intention is never to harm another soul but to tell a story of personal redemption. My hope is that *The Tell* offers inspiration and encouragement regarding life's challenges, including exceptional and extraordinary ones. I also pray each of us receives the grace we need to face each new day, whatever it may bring.

Jia Apple

I dedicate this book to my three daughters.
My heart sings with love for you.

"Am I dead yet?"

—Dr. Suess

ACKNOWLEDGEMENTS

I sincerely thank all who helped me along *The Tell*'s journey.

I thank my daughters for their ideas and challenges regarding this work. You continue to inspire me daily.

Special thanks go to my first-draft editor and dear friend, Barbara Bennett, for encouraging me to explore an unorthodox idea of presenting the life story of Jubilee Given. What started as a second memoir then took the shape of a book of days about the endearing character Jubilee.

Profound thanks go to Judy Reagan for reading my first draft and offering endless support, feedback, and encouragement. You have been the tether to my kite, and I love you dearly. Thank you hardly seems enough to express my gratitude.

Dr. Ponder Goddard, so many thanks go to you. Thank you for being a sounding board these past few years and offering me the support I needed to not give up on this project. In the busiest of times, you directed me back to my voice and my truth. I could not have made this book what it is without your help as my Reader's Advocate. Your edits and strong suggestions about what my readers should be asked to endure have been invaluable. Lastly, but not nearly enough, you helped me find my protagonist's name, Jubilee Given. May we always have the courage to come out of hiding so we can be the recipient and giver of life's grace and forgiveness.

Kristi, thank you for trying to get through the manuscript and for the original cover clothesline idea. You're an amazing creative and a black heart sister through and through.

My enduring gratitude goes out to Tina Kimpo. She spent hours editing, combing through passages, asking questions to bring clarity, and fine-tuning Jubilee's message with me.

To Amanda and the Awaken Village Press team and your ability to take a finished manuscript and make it better. To James and Alan for reading my *for real* final draft and for your uplifting endorsements, and again, Kristi and your goddess mother energy, I love so much … *cha cha cha.*

As any author will tell you, each written creation is a journey of the soul, done with the harmony and contribution of others. Thank you all so much.

INTRODUCTION

Jubilee Given was born in the small rural town of Oakley, Indiana, on October 3, 1959. The white clapboard house was a three-bedroom, one-bath ranch. Within the quarter-acre yard, there was luscious green grass, a variety of flowers, a cherry tree, and an apple tree. In the backyard, there was a clothesline, a tool shed, a fire barrel for burning trash, a garbage heap, and a garden plot. Behind the property were acres of cornfields, a majestic oak tree, and a tall, slender hickory nut tree. Beyond the cornfields were the woods. This was the playground Jubilee explored.

Jubilee was the eighth of ten children born to Iris and Gordon Given, so there was already a "way" for the placement and treatment of children by the time Jubilee was born. When a baby arrived at the Given family, it stayed in the crib in "Mom and Dad's" room until the age of three or until the bars of the crib could no longer keep the baby confined. There were also the girls' room and the boys' room, each with one full-sized bed, where three girls and three boys slept, respectively. Later on, Dad built another room in the basement for the two oldest. The old house seemed to fit everyone in their time, albeit like sardines in a can.

The house was newly built just months before Jubilee's birth. The older children remember the house up the same street where they lived that was even closer to the railroad tracks, and the even older children remember the farm before that. Each residence brought with it memories of the unique life it held.

Jubilee's mother was born Iris Heartwise in Lewisburg, Kentucky, in 1920. Iris was one of fourteen children, and because of the time in which she lived, she watched several of her siblings die as children and then later as adults. By the time of Iris's death, she was the last surviving member of her immediate family. She survived her childhood illnesses but fell victim to rape, wartime depression, and poverty. In spite of these challenges, Iris was able to teach herself guitar, harmonica, and keyboards. She and her brother sang together at social functions, such as barn dances and local community gatherings, and rose to local popularity and demand. In addition to being a singer and musician, Iris dreamed of going to trade school and becoming a businesswoman. Her family eventually moved to Indiana, and this is where, in the spring of 1940, she married her childhood friend and sweetheart, Gordon Given.

Gordon was born in Indiana in 1920 and was the fifth of six children. Not much is known about his early life other than his excellent athleticism and his volatile temper. His reputation for being mischievous and quick-tempered created an air of fear around him. Like many other men of his day, Gordon farmed and worked on automobiles.

Gordon and Iris began their lives together as most other couples, and as fate would have it, Iris soon became pregnant. Neither Gordon's nor Iris's families were religious folk, but this was soon to change, as they both experienced a conversion to Christianity early in their marriage and gave their lives over to Jesus Christ as their lord and savior.

By 1959, the year of Jubilee's birth, Iris had fallen into a spiraling decline of mental illness. Iris cultivated an extreme devotion to God through churchgoing, prayer, and biblical saturation, and although this served to provide her strength and guidance, the characters of God and the Devil also became the voices of her schizophrenic world. It is likely but still speculation that Gordon's violent temper and sexual promiscuity made Iris's condition worse.

Then, Jubilee was born. Jubilee was largely raised by her two oldest sisters and, as a toddler, was unsure who her real mother was. Iris was often visiting friends or family for her "health" or in asylums for the mentally insane for weeks or even months at a time. When Iris was there, Jubilee was exposed to an extreme degree of uncertainty about the nature and safety of her life. This intermingled with the seemingly normal times of laughter, prayer, singing, and lightheartedness. Jubilee saw her dad as a god among men. He seemed good, trustworthy, and strong. He was a fire chief, a deacon in the church, a provider, and someone who tied her shoes and carried her in his arms. He loved her and cared for her in the absence of a vacant mother. This was her reality until he showed the ugly face of his rage and began touching her in ways that caused her to feel uncomfortable. Then, Dad became a man to be feared.

After Jubilee, two more children were born, making ten. Iris's body and mind were all but used up, and Gordon was still the same man. His violence and sexual deviance were directed toward his children and, presumably, his wife.

Jubilee had nowhere to turn. Her safe places were her siblings, but they were also victims, and when it was their time to leave home, they fled. They all fled. Jubilee was left waiting until it could be her time to run, but to where? Most of her siblings went on to college—the boys to stay out of Vietnam and the girls to find husbands. The years of dodging her parents left Jubilee in search of a way to find relief.

Jubilee developed the ability to induce herself into hypnotic trances by the time she was fourteen years old. It seemed to come so naturally to her, and soon she was folding time and space into herself in such a way that all fear, pain, and uncertainty lifted off her like a feather ... but only temporarily. Near the same time, she began lucid dreaming and, at night, awoke to see entities standing in her bedroom. This was alarming and frightened her, but these phenomena followed her throughout her life.

At the age of seventeen, Jubilee went to the same college some of her siblings attended. It was a Bible college associated with their church. After one and a half years, Jubilee dropped out due to failed attendance and drug use. She eventually got clean and tried to return to college but dropped out once again. She struggled with depression and anxiety with suicidal ideation that continued to go untreated.

In 1980, Jubilee reunited with the preacher's son from her home church, and they married. She was married to him for eleven years and had three daughters. Not long after the birth of her third daughter, a friend of Jubilee asked her to attend a class where a talented teacher was presenting. Jubilee was entranced by the teaching of this man, Jerry, and went on to attend three series of his classes. Soon Jerry and his wife and daughter were socializing together as friends with Jubilee and her family.

Jerry offered Jubilee and her friend jobs working for his company, where he gently interjected personal guidance, emotional support, and spiritual wisdom. Eventually, Jerry rose to be someone admired, respected, trusted, and thought to be a divine being with great authority. Once this trust was gained with Jubilee, he also required sex, companionship, and complete obedience. These stages of grooming and cultic activities swept Jubilee out of her marriage and her home and into another life over the span of fourteen years. Jubilee was physically separated from her children for two years, her siblings for ten years, and her parents for eleven years. It was her own personal hell that she was compelled to experience because a god-man told her this sacrifice would ultimately save them all.

Then, the house of Jerry's making began to crumble. Jubilee discovered some of Jerry's lies, and the trust that was once there faltered. Then, in 1999, Jubilee's middle daughter, Molly, committed suicide. At her funeral, Jubilee was reunited with her siblings and began to long for the lost life with her family. Coupled with the ongoing deceptions, degradations, and abuse from Jerry, Jubilee began the journey of finding her way to a life she could call her own.

On January 9, 2004, Jubilee's brothers came with a moving truck and helped her leave that life behind.

Jubilee's life of freedom has offered her a chance to find out what works and what doesn't. For decades, she had been coerced to deny her own nature because it was an abomination to God. She now identifies as a lesbian.

On August 15, 2014, Jubilee experienced extreme trauma-oriented dissociation when she received news of Jerry's violent death by suicide. Shortly after Jerry's death, Jubilee was the victim of a unique spinal injury, and, beyond all odds and with no known treatment, she fought for her own healing. Living with these psychological and physical hardships has demanded a presence of mind and forced Jubilee to grasp hold of her life.

Jubilee was raised as a Christian, but in the course of her healing journey, she discovered and connected to her Native American heritage. Reclaiming the spiritual practice of her ancestors has given her something she can believe in.

She is a mother, a grandmother, and a teacher of art. She is an inspiration and comfort to those who have also lost children, and she longs to be a vessel of encouragement and wisdom to the abused, neglected, and struggling souls of this planet. Jubilee is a miracle that speaks to the miracle in each person who has had to struggle for survival.

In *The Tell,* you will read unique memories from this story. Each day is a moment in time that reflects the experiences from the life of Jubilee Given.

CAST OF CHARACTERS
(IN CHRONOLOGICAL ORDER)

JUBILEE'S PARENTS
Iris Heartwise and Gordon Given

JUBILEE'S SIBLINGS
Daniel, Jennifer, Barbara, Jesse, Mark, Jill, Doug,
Sam, and Mindy

JUBILEE'S HUSBAND
Granger

JUBILEE'S DAUGHTERS
Hannah, Molly, and Simone

JUBILEE'S GRANDCHILDREN
Clark, Charles, Wednesday, Sonja, Luna, and Reese

RELIGIOUS CULT MEMBERS
Leader–Jerry
Jerry's wife and daughter–Tamra and Jordan
(other members not mentioned)

JUBILEE'S FIRST WIFE
Dee

JUBILEE'S SECOND WIFE
Lorraine

LORRAINE'S EX-WIFE
Linda

JUBILEE'S FRIENDS
Arlene and Kitty, Bob

JUBILEE'S BUSINESS PARTNER AND BEST FRIEND
Tory

JUBILEE'S GIRLFRIEND
Abra

JUBILEE'S DOGS
Trouble, Nan, and Jasper

PROLOGUE

Hi, my name is Jubilee Given.

This book is a collection of memories that span the course of my life, which I have organized and condensed into one calendar year. As the calendar year unfolds, these moments tell the truth about what I have experienced on any given day of my life on this Earth.

This work is not a fluid story or a lovely symphony with clear crescendos and diminuendos that ease the reader into a satisfying climax and gracious landing, but life is often like this, no? In my experience, one day might be blissful and the next an event could rock me to my core. As much as I might try to string my life into a neat and simple tale, the actual living of my days has not been like that. My stories are offered here in the knowledge that no matter what life may give you, even death in its varied forms, there is more life to come.

Though unconventional in format, this memoir is all about getting up every day and facing life as it is, come what may. In my experience, sometimes life just doesn't work out, and it is in enduring our uncertain days and continuing to walk forward through the mire of what life can be like that we will eventually find ourselves. I did it, and you can too.

I am Jubilee Given. And with a humble heart, I offer you my days.

Winter

Reflections on Winter

SACRED NORTH

From Winter comes the final look upon my life. She comes from the North and is my true mother. Her hair is raven black with braids upon her shoulders. She wears a white buckskin dress with beads clicking together at the bottom of long strands. She doesn't hesitate to approach me with kind eyes and a welcoming smile. With all of her knowing, she shows me my lessons one last time.

Winter is Grandmother moon shining upon the freshly fallen snow that makes the night as day. Her wisdom is gathered from every other season as she ponders me now. Closing my eyes, I smell her northerly wind. There is a fire in the hearth burning away my dross. Winter is my home .... It is here where I begin, and now she has prepared a place for me to rest.

DECEMBER 21

California, 1981, age 22

It's the first day of winter, the shortest day of the year, and the longest night in the Northern Hemisphere. The numbers suggest a mirror or a palindrome. Some say the world will end on this day in 2012, but I don't believe it. I have just given birth to my daughter, Hannah. She is the most beautiful little person I have ever seen. She came from me, and holding her is the most miraculous thing I can ever imagine doing. Seeing her face and her eyes looking into my own is the most transcendent and sacred experience I have ever had. It is as though she is peering into my being. She has a key to me. Now I know what it's like to create another human being and to give birth. This sacred bond between us ensures that life goes on. I want nothing more than to be with her. She is completely dependent upon me and wants only to be with me. She is simply perfect, and I love her.

DECEMBER 22

California, 1981, age 22

I am pretty sure I know very little about taking care of a baby. I've never been a mom before; how do I take care of this being? My emotions are raw. Will I know what she needs? Somehow just holding her close to me feels as though it helps, but I am listening to the nurse's instructions in the next cubicle, where she is telling the other new mother things that no one has mentioned to me. All my life, I have learned from listening to others' conversations, watching what others are doing, and observing my surroundings. Now another life is dependent on my getting it right. It's no longer enough to learn only from watching others; I must educate myself and learn the right way to be. I need to listen to myself and trust myself. I don't want to let my baby down.

Jubilee tip: Don't be afraid to ask questions.

DECEMBER 23

California, 1981, age 22

As I hold my tiny baby girl, I feel like nothing else exists but us. Each of my senses is focused on her. It is as though I am holding my heart wrapped in a warm blanket. I look at her wanting nothing, and she gives me everything in return. My heart is alive, and I know that I would rise like a tiger to protect her innocence and beauty. We are both in this world to walk an uncertain path, and yet, at this moment, nothing is more certain to me than the unity I feel with my baby. I want her to have every good thing, and I want to give them to her. I want her to have a better start than I did.

DECEMBER 24

Connecticut, 1991, age 32

Jerry is my teacher, and I try very hard to follow his instructions, but fear and grief paralyze me. My three daughters have been taken from me, and I feel a despair for which there are no words. My heart is shattered. I am not alive. I am walking every moment as a dead woman, and no words console me. Jerry said I should let them go because my sacrifice will please God. Why would God ask this of me?
Jubilee tip: Sometimes God isn't really God at all.

DECEMBER 25

Connecticut, 1992, age 33

Today is Christmas, and I am devoid of joy. The gifts I receive mean nothing to me. All I want is to be with my girls. Jerry says that I can't call them. He says that I must be strong, and I will be rewarded by God. He says God is pleased with my obedience.

I pleaded with him. I wept. I've never been without my children on Christmas day, and I told him how much I missed them. He said God gave up His child for the world and His son was put to death, so my sacrifice is really small. He insists I must trust that what he is saying is true, but it's Christmas day and I am not with my children. They are the only gift I want.

DECEMBER 26

Indiana, 1969, age 10

This pogo stick is amazing. I am working on 100 jumps in a row without falling off. It's pretty cold outside, but I don't care. If I stay on the porch, it's way easier because the porch is made of concrete and is smooth. So far, I am up to seventy-three jumps without falling off. I'm sure I can do it eventually, but I just got it for Christmas yesterday, so I haven't had all that much time to practice. I love this thing.

Jubilee tip: Goals are good.

DECEMBER 27

Indiana, 1975, age 16

The snow is falling hard, and I am sitting here watching it. Any other person would be content to be warm and inside, but I wish I had someplace to be other than here. In my mind, I journey outside and walk. Everyone else has gone to sleep, but I'm restless. The Christmas tree is still standing, and it's still beautiful, but now the needles are brittle and falling. On New Year's Day, someone will take it down. I'm stranded in the doorway of decision, thinking of leaving home, feeling I have all the power in the world and yet not a clue how to use it. The urge to go is so strong, but I have no money. I seem to be at the mercy of others who might or might not help me.

Jubilee tip: Get a job.

DECEMBER 28

Minnesota, 1984, age 25

The snow has drifted at least ten feet beside the condo. It is now so cold outside that there's a risk of frostbite within minutes of exposure. My daughters, Hannah and Molly, are playing in their room upstairs, and my husband, Granger, has gone out to the store. It's beautiful outside, and the sun's light makes it deceptively inviting. I can see the colors of the light reflecting off the snow in the minutest sparkles of tiny rainbows. The warmth inside our home keeps me content. Is there a homeless person out there in the cold? I know there is. God help them stay safe.

I'm going to make something delicious and warm, maybe cookies or hot chocolate. Hannah and Molly will love it, and we'll sit in the warmth of the rays coming through the window panes watching tiny rainbows.

DECEMBER 29

New Mexico, 2016, age 57

Winter is a place of comfort for me. I live in the high desert of New Mexico, where the sun shines and the sky tells a new story every day. I sit in my prayer circle and watch the ravens soar above me. The ravens know me. Last week, there was an attack in the night, and a raven was lost. It may have been a coyote or even an owl. I gave her a proper burial, but her mate still looks for her. My heart is sad, yet I know it's the way of things. I know this very well.

I look to the north within my medicine wheel, and I see my spiritual mother there. She is beautiful with her long black hair and dark skin. In my eyes, she is younger than me, yet she is old enough to have given birth to me. Her dress is white buckskin, trimmed in beaded braids with long hanging strands. She looks into my eyes and lovingly smiles at me. We know each other's hearts, and I am profoundly comfortable sitting in her presence. I can speak of anything to her, and she will listen and give me her best. Here I know I am accepted, loved, and cherished.

DECEMBER 30 (1)

Oregon, 2020, age 61

This year is nearing an end, and the people on this planet have been through so much. We are all hoping we have come through the worst of this plague. The isolation and fear are hard to bear, and no one seems to know what is yet to come. COVID-19 has nearly killed some of my family. So far, we have stayed alive, but there is no doubt that this virus is deadly. Prayer has become a staple of life for the Given family, and the internet is our only means to connect. This is no way to live ... but at least we're alive.

DECEMBER 31

New Mexico, 2014, age 55

The spirit of the North comes to me in my depths. She escorts me on many dream journeys. She shows me magical things and takes me to places I cannot otherwise reach. She is my potential and my most distant past. She is my present moment and the moments yet to be. She is life in all its terror and beauty, and she knows all my secrets. My gift to her is my soul.

JANUARY 1

Colorado, 2008, age 48

Lorraine and her partner hosted a party at their big log cabin house today to ring in the new year. Dee and I were there along with our new friends, Arlene and Kitty. We also met two new gals who work as guards at the Denver Women's Correctional Facility. Everyone here is queer except for Bob, who lives next door in a smaller log cabin. He's a kind man with a strong presence, and he came toting cigars and bourbon. He used to be a cop in Colorado Springs until he got shot in the line of duty—and, well, I think that would stop anyone from that profession. He also used to be one of the guards for the Tomb of the Unknown Soldier. The Tomb of the Unknown Soldier is in Arlington

National Cemetery and is guarded twenty-four hours a day. I find this very fascinating.

Kitty and Lorraine manned the turkey fryer in the driveway, and everyone had a drink in their hands except for me and Dee, who is twelve years sober now. I joined her in sobriety at the beginning of our relationship. We are the only two non-drinkers present, and as the day goes by, I feel as though everything gets louder, sloppier, and more exaggerated ..... I am a spectator among my own friends. They're like circus performers teetering about and pretending it's all part of the show ... a really big show.

That said, I really enjoyed smoking a good cigar with Bob. That was fun, but I'm certain that Lorraine should never smoke a cigar again because she turned a kind of light gray-green and got sick as a dog.

We had a great time with our new friends, and the fried bird was the most deliciously moist turkey I have ever had in my life. A beautiful time had by lovely people. I think these folks will be my friends for a very long time ... at least I hope so.

JANUARY 2

Indiana, 1977, age 17

New Year's Eve started out as heaven but ended as hell. It was pretty cool to be invited to the teacher-student party. The teachers I love were there and also my friends from art class. I never drank alcohol before, so I was excited to try it. The first drink felt like someone poured liquid bliss all over me. I had never felt that way before. It was as if all the concerns and bad feelings of my life just lifted off me. I did what I thought anyone would do: I drank everything and anything I could get my hands on.

One of my art friends cautioned me that maybe I shouldn't drink too much, but I couldn't understand why. Others at the party looked concerned about me—teachers and students—but I felt amazing. When we finally left the party and headed to my friend Dawn's house, my world spun uncontrollably. I landed on

Dawn's bed and suddenly realized I was not okay. I spent most of the evening with my head over a trash can. I swear I never knew this would happen. There is no way I will ever do this again. I hate that I don't seem to know anything about the world and the way it works.

Jubilee tip: Don't mix alcohols, and stop at two drinks.

JANUARY 3

Connecticut, 1993, age 33

I walk down the drive where I live now and turn left to start my short walk down to the water's edge. I take another left when I get to the Victorian house. I walk by, acknowledging the old trees in the yard. I see my pink rock ahead, half-submerged in the water, and I walk toward it. It's my rock, and I go there to cry. We have an agreement, this stone and me—it's taking the weight of my hopeless tears. I've come to call it the crying rock. I've come to love it in the way we love the things that carry our burdens.

I have lost my three children, and I am nothing without them. My tears roll over the pink stone, fall upon the water of the Thames, and head to the ocean. If only I could begin again, I would not be taking this walk. I am sacrificing myself so that others may live. I've been told there is a greater purpose. I have no joy, and no solace makes this journey bearable. With God as my witness, I am making these choices for Him.

Jubilee tip: Think hard about making sacrifices for God. There's usually a man behind it.

JANUARY 4

New Mexico, 2014, age 54

I stand before the cold winds of the north and listen to this familiar voice speak to me ...

"Come, daughter, are you afraid of me?" She asks, *"Are you afraid that your life is nothing? Do you worry that you're a failure? There's so much I want*

to share with you. I feel your longing, and I hear your cries. I want you as you want me and even more. Come near, come close, don't judge any longer, and don't dare think less of yourself. I don't. Hear me now, sit in the perfect place. Yes, the perfect place. You, Jubilee, are that perfect place. You are enough, and I love you."

JANUARY 5
Indiana, 1968, age 8

We just had the biggest snow I can ever remember. School was closed today, so my brother Doug and I are taking the sled to the sledding hill in the woods. We ran out of heat last night in the house, so Dad had the oven door open to heat up the kitchen and dining room when we got up. I call it the kitchen campfire. I like real fire better, but this is pretty cool since we are inside the house and cold. It's happened before, but the heat always comes back on eventually. Mom says we ran out of money, but she knows God will help us. He always seems to pull through for Mom. She said He promised to provide for those who pay their tithe. That means ten percent of Dad's paycheck goes to the church every week. Mom always gives money to God first, even if she knows the heat will go out.

Doug and I will put on at least three layers of clothes before we head out to the sledding hill. We'll take some matches to make a fire too.

Jubilee tip: Pay God, no matter what.

JANUARY 6 (2)
Oregon, 2021, age 61

Today a group of crazy-ass Trump supporters stormed the Capitol building. As far as I know, Congress had convened to confirm the vote for President of the United States, but the Trump folks were convinced it was all a fraud. MAGA flags were flying as an enraged mob pushed through the Capitol doors. They threatened our Congress, and people lost their lives. It was a tragic day in our nation's history, as our very own President Trump instigated and fueled this riot. It makes me feel sick and a little afraid to know that we elected a man like this and that he willfully tried to overthrow our government.

JANUARY 7

Connecticut, 2004, age 44

My brothers are on their way to get me. I've done all I can to get ready. The rest just needs to unfold. The bond between Jerry and me has been broken enough for my escape. The plan is for my brothers to come and get a room for the night, contact the police to tell them what they are about to do but to maintain strict confidentiality for my safety ... in two days they'll wait for my signal and then come and get me. I'm afraid, but I know I have to walk through this to have a chance to live again. I must do this, and then I'll be free.

JANUARY 8

Connecticut, 2004, age 44

I heard from my brothers. They're in town after driving all night. They're here to liberate me. This house feels so alien to me now. What was once a captive's cell has no power to hold me any longer. I prayed through the night for safe passage, ignoring Jerry's pounding on the ceiling demanding that I take my place on the floor beside him. I ignored the incessant calls to come and be the subservient consort he trained me to be. It is the winter of my obedience, and I am no longer obliged to follow this false god. Tomorrow I walk a free woman.

JANUARY 9

Connecticut, 2004, age 44

I planned my exit for today because it is shopping day. For the past several years, we've shopped every Friday. We get up, we get ready, and we all go together. Today, I am not going. It is the first time I have not gone, and I'm certain they all know that when they return, I will not be waiting for them. My captor and his wife and child stand and look at me with dismay in their eyes.

Once I am gone, I expect he will call me a whore ... a thief, and a villain. It is very likely he will try and have me killed because of what I know. I don't care. If I stayed here I would die anyway. It's been fourteen years of captivity, brainwashing, sexual abuse, grueling abasement, and manipulative control. All under the guise of saving me, my family, and my children from the wrath of God. I am declaring him a liar. And I'm leaving.

JANUARY 10

Indiana, 1965, age 5

They took Mom away again today. My sister said Mom had to go somewhere where she could feel better. Mom gets such a painful look in her eyes when she is feeling bad. I hate the way I feel when they take her from home. My big sisters, Jennifer and Barbara, are here to watch us kids, but I worry about Mom. I hate to see her feel so bad. If she were here, I would rub lotion on her legs. She always feels better when I do that for her. She loves it when I comb her hair too. When she gets home, I will do that for her. I hope she comes home soon.

JANUARY 11

Connecticut, 2004, age 44

My brothers came and got me and as much as we could fit in the truck. We had to leave a lot of my stuff behind. My adrenaline was high, and I was so afraid Jerry would double back and decide to fight to keep me from my escape.

Leaving Tamra and Jordan breaks my heart because I know life will be more difficult for them without me. Tamra is my friend, and Jordan is like a daughter to me. I hope that watching me find my freedom will help them understand how they can, too, if they choose.

My brothers created a sleeping space in the front of the moving truck, and we all lay one beside another as they took turns sleeping and driving through the night. We didn't stop until we arrived this morning back in Indiana, my home place. I'm staying with my brother Mark for now. For the first time in fourteen years, Jerry can't get to me.

This feeling I have is surreal. Am I in a dream? I am breathing for the first time in so long.

I kneel and place my palms flat upon the earth. It's cold and hard, but I love it. I lower my head to smell the winter grass, and I kiss the ground. I am free.

JANUARY 12

New Mexico, 2015, age 55

Last night I had the most vivid dream. I was standing inside one of the great pyramids of Egypt. There was an Egyptian man wearing a hat standing beside me. He was perplexed because he couldn't find a way to open one of the inner chambers. I looked at him and asked if he wanted my help because I knew how to open it. He said yes, so I began. First, I picked up a short stone wand, the color of the sea, then I broke it into two pieces and placed the ends of each piece into the indentations on the wall. As I did this, the massive wall moved in a circular motion, like a scene from an Indiana Jones film. The wall opened into a chamber, releasing a gust of wind that rushed through me with such force that it lifted me up into the air. My arms were spread wide, and my head tilted backward. As I elevated, I felt myself transforming, and as I floated back down to the floor, I saw my skin had turned blue. Then a line of people extended past a doorway to my right, waiting to see me. Some I knew and some I didn't, but they were all there for the same thing. They were there to be healed by me. My daughter, Hannah, stood in line. I intuitively knew what she needed when I wrapped my arms around her. As I held her, we both floated up into the air, turning slowly in a clockwise direction. Soon afterward, I awoke from the dream.

"Lorraine!" I exclaimed to my wife.

"Yes"

"I dreamed I was a blue healer."

"You dreamed you were a dog?"

"Ha! No, I dreamed I was a healer, and I was blue. It was amazing."

Jubilee tip: Pay close attention to your dreams.

JANUARY 13

Colorado, 2019, age 59

> Before I sleep, between the hot and cold of things, I simmer
> Snow devils dance around and drift
> This station watching, impervious to expectation, listening
> Fighting impulse to influence while judging the sharp edge
> Desirous of all
> Hearing the rise and fall of my beloved, I rest

JANUARY 14

Indiana, 1976, age 16

It seems like the only person on the planet who gives a damn about me is my art teacher. She has done so much, and I can't begin to tell you what an angel of light she is to me. My workload at school has been really heavy because I'm involved in a lot of after-school music, drama, and art commitments. Most days, I don't have the money to eat, so I hang out in the art department during lunch. Ms. G sees me a lot and tries to get me to eat, but I feel like I can't take her money. Lately, she's offered me jobs to do at her house on the weekends so I can earn enough money to buy lunch, but there are a lot of days I am at school until late, having not eaten all day, and then go home late to who knows what. It's not easy. If it wasn't for Ms. G, I would be completely sunk. She is the one who suggested I take baths more often and start wearing deodorant. She's also the one who made sure I had eyeglasses so I could see the board at school, and she made sure I had an alarm clock so I could get to school on time. She even gives me rides home. It's so weird to have someone actually care about my life and offer to do things for me. I know that must sound strange, but no one has ever shown an interest in helping me before. There must be a special place in heaven for people like her. She really is a good person.

JANUARY 15

Connecticut, 1992, age 32

Jerry genuinely seems to care about me, and he understands that the truth about God is the most important thing to me. I have an open door to Jerry's knowledge, and it's a true gift and privilege. Jerry's teachings reflect his intellect and close personal relationship with God, and I admire that. His authority and wisdom are other-worldly. He has extraordinary visions and experiences, and some of them are much like the ones I have had. The thirst and longing in my heart to know God and understand His ways are my breath and lifeblood. The thing I want most in life is to know the truth of God, and I would do almost anything for that.

JANUARY 16

Indiana, 1968, age 8

The house is quiet, but I can't go to sleep. My sister is lying beside me, and I'm pretty sure she's asleep. The room is dark. I can hear my mother snoring. My eyes focus on the empty space of the dark. There are little specs that look like invisible rain, and I can see the way it flows and shifts. I wonder what it is? In the distance, I can hear the train coming, and I'm guessing it just blew the whistle for Sunnyside Road. I wonder if it is always the same train that just goes back and forth in front of our house. Pretty soon, it will get here and rattle our furniture. No one ever wakes up because we're all used to it. The lights will race across my room, and it will blow its horn for the intersection at Oakland Road. It happens every time. I'll count and see how long it takes to get here. 1 … 2 … 3 … 4 … 5 …

JANUARY 17

Oregon, 2021, age 61

Every creative thought is a newborn baby in someone's arms.

JANUARY 18

Oregon, 2021, age 61

Every day, there is news of more deaths from this global pandemic. It has swept over this planet, and so many are struggling. I've lost one friend, and Long COVID continues to plague several of my family members. There are no public gatherings; everyone is wearing masks, or at least should be, and everyone is afraid. People look at each other differently now. What is happening? I see fearful eyes from behind masks. I check myself and wonder if I'm transmitting the same fear. I know I am.

I'm learning to smile with my eyes more.

Jubilee tip: Wash your hands.

JANUARY 19

Colorado, 2008, age 48

Last night, as I was falling asleep, I got a realistic sensation of being cut off from myself or parts of myself. It was an odd feeling. A force entered me and separated the two hemispheres of my brain. Then, I saw myself holding each half in my hands, standing in that space between thoughts. It felt as though I existed with no outside influences. The only dilemma was what to do with these brain halves in my hands. I put them back together and re-entered my body as I drifted away. It was easy, and I don't remember anything after that.

JANUARY 20

Indiana 1962, age 2

This piano is so big; luckily, I have this round stool. The top of the stool turns round and round, and then it stops. I can pull myself up on top and stand up. Once I do that, I can close the piano lid and climb over the keys. I put a pillow on the floor, and when I jump off the piano, I land on it with my diapered bottom. I love the sound it makes when I hit the pillow. My rubber pants make a squishing sound. It is so much fun that I laugh, get up, and do it all over again.

JANUARY 21 (3)

Connecticut, 2003, age 43

This morning, I awoke from a vivid dream. It feels as if I am being warned. I'm not sure what to make of it.

I dreamed a train came, and I saw there were dark shadows inside of it. People were wearing overcoats and hats, and they were unsure of where they were going. Someone told them they were going to a safe place, but I knew it was the death train. Not all people were part of the death train, but if you were picked up, death was inevitable. Select people, lower castes, undesirables, and people of specific religions were taken. The train was long and crowded.

When I saw the death train coming for me, I ran. As the guards chased me, motion sensors triggered an assault of sound and vibration. I heard a booming voice repeatedly say, "You cannot escape," and simultaneously, the sound vibrations assaulted my body to implant me with cancer. I felt sound and energy penetrate all around me, but I outran it. I ran hard and escaped.

Then, I found myself on the train, looking for a way to escape again. *If I don't get off now, I never will.* The guards chased me as I jumped off the train and ran into a large, old building. Inside, there was a group of people waiting for a meeting to begin. I noticed a sick man lying on the floor. I asked if I could hide by taking his seat, and he told me where to go. I entered the meeting area in his place to hide among the many. Soon, someone noticed that I didn't belong there, so I quietly left. Everywhere I went in my dream, the train found me. This time, Jerry was driving the train. He was one of the death squad members, and I was afraid of him.

I then met a family standing next to the train, and they handed me their baby. As I held her, I realized this baby was my deceased child, Molly. Jerry asked for the baby, and I was so afraid of him that I handed her over. She laughed at Jerry's funny faces, and then he handed her back to me. Turning back to the family, I returned the baby. I instantly began missing her, but I knew it was for the best. In a low and quiet voice, Jerry looked into my eyes and said, "Get me all of the babies."

"No," I said.

The dream ended.

JANUARY 22

Connecticut, 1989, age 29

My husband and I were in bed this morning. I woke up while he was still sleeping and saw a man sitting at the end of our bed. He had blonde wavy hair, and I felt as though I knew him, so I said hello. He didn't say anything at all or even flinch. It was as though he were sitting guard like a sentinel. I decided to lie back down, and I fell back to sleep. Upon waking this morning, I have a strong feeling that it was an angel, and his name is Raphael. I do wonder what he wanted and why he didn't speak to me. I was so happy to see him.

Jubilee tip: Not everyone speaks with their voice.

JANUARY 23

Oregon, 2021, age 61

Today, beside Lithia Creek, these comforting words, maybe God, washed through me:

"Does it surprise you that I speak to you so easily? Listening is so important. Once you stop to hear Me, here I am. There is so much to hear. The water, of course, is easy to hear, but what of the trees? The moss? What about you? What are you saying to all these living things and to the people in your life? All beings are listening to each other in turn, including you. What is your essence saying?

What is your resting state saying? This vibrational essence carries a message all its own. The trees, the water, the rocks, and the people all hear and feel it and are speaking too.

"The air itself has this life. It is My life. Give your breath as food and take Mine to nourish you. The trees will know you, and so will I. It is to your advantage to secure your place in Me so we may all assist you in your hour of need. We have consumed your thoughts and deeds ahead of your needs. If then in purity you live, then in purity you will thrive and die."

Jubilee tip: Listen to everything.

JANUARY 24

Ohio, 2020, age 60

Today, I witnessed my beloved brother-in-law transition through the veil we must all pass through. His loving family surrounded his body … my sister Barbara and his three loving children were all there holding him as he walked into a new life.

Be brave, fine man, and find your place with our ancestors. Keep us in your strong care, and know we will join you when our time comes. You are so loved.

JANUARY 25

New Mexico, 2016, age 56

My wife was lying in bed next to me early this morning. Suddenly, she jumped up and said,

"Oh, my god! There's a spider!"

I sprung out of bed and watched as she feverishly looked for a giant spider she said had fallen from the ceiling. I knew at that moment that she was seeing an unphysical being.

I lay back in bed and smiled.

"Welcome to my world, sweetheart."

Of course, her response was astonishment.

"No, really. I saw it!"

I simply said, "Believe me, I know. Just wait until the devil shows up."

Winter

JANUARY 26

California, 2028, age 68

The ten Given siblings are remarkable souls. Today, I am reflecting on what we have overcome as a family. Aside from the terror of my mother's schizophrenia, I still am in awe of the serial damage my father did and didn't do to this family. He really was a brutal man, and we're good people in spite of him. To my knowledge, he never made a confession because he was not the kind of man who could admit he was wrong. Repentance is a turning of direction to then walk in another direction. My dad enjoyed his bad behavior too much to ever do this. He believed he was entitled to it.

I used to believe he held redeeming qualities and this somehow balanced his abusive acts, but I no longer think this. I'm still perplexed that he was able to harm innocent souls and think nothing of it. In my lifetime, I've seen evidence of many men like this. Some in charge of nations. When will it ever stop?

JANUARY 27

Indiana, 1969, age 9

I had to teach a kid a lesson at school today. His name is Walter, and he is a jerk. I was getting a drink from the water fountain, and he pushed my head into it, causing me to hit my lip. I turned around and grabbed him with both hands by his collar, pulled him halfway off the floor, and ripped a button off his shirt. He started crying, and I told him never to do that again. Not ever. I hope he learned his lesson.

Jubilee tip: Don't fuck with strong girls.

JANUARY 28 (4)

Rhode Island, 1986, age 26

Today, I was excited to watch the Space Shuttle Challenger take off for its mission. Everything about the take-off and the first minute of flight seemed normal. But after seventy-three seconds, the ship exploded. Right on the television, I watched as seven crew members vanished with their ship. I was horrified. In a moment, a flash of time … they were there, and then they were gone. Life is so fragile it makes me shudder.

JANUARY 29

Colorado, 2009, age 49

My mother died today at eighty-eight years old. I'm in Colorado and unable to get to her, so I talked through the phone so she could hear me.

"Mom, I love you. Don't worry about Dad. We'll take care of him. Don't be afraid, Mom. I love you so much."

My sister told me Mom heard me, and I believe she did. She's gone now. Who is going to pray for us kids? I swear Mom's prayers kept us alive so much of the time. In her prayers, we always came first. I think this is one of the reasons her prayers meant so much to us. She couldn't tend to us kids as a healthy mom, but she was the most epic praying mother ever. Thank you, Mom, thank you so much. I love you.

JANUARY 30

Colorado, 2009, age 49

Yesterday I listened over the phone, as my mother died and my siblings sang, *By and By*. She's left us, and all that remains is the lonely shell of her body. Where's mom? Did she really love that song so much that it was the last thing she wanted to hear, or did we just not know what else to do?

She loved to hear her children sing most of all. Somehow, it made her feel closer to God and believe that her children would somehow stay safe if they just kept singing … about God.

How does a person just disappear? By and by, as the song goes, we will understand it all better. I just want to know where my mom is—I need to know this.

Winter

JANUARY 31

New Mexico, 2013, age 53

I've often wondered how it is that I can receive impressions for people that are so relevant to their lives. The images that sweep through my mind's eye tell an intimate story. I bring these images to life through my art, and then I tell them the meaning as it comes to me.

Today, I had a vision of myself—from a past life, I think. It was me, and I was older and plumper. I wore layers of materials that didn't match, and they were old and faded. Purple and yellow flowers were woven into the fabric of the scarf tied around my head. I was blind to the physical world, but the spirit world was something that I saw clearly. I saw myself sitting in a room at a wooden table; I was surrounded by old riff-raff collected over time. The light was dim, and a tin can sat on the table in front of me. This is how I made a living. I was the picture seer. Here I saw the pictures of people's lives as they came to sit across from me at this table, dropping money in the can and bringing me food.

In my vision, a man came to see me. His clothes were clean and neat, and his hair was the lightest brown. As my seeing hands went to his face, I felt him searching and yearning to know more about his life. His face was smooth, and he was young. Then I saw for him … I saw a ship upon the sea … and the clouds of a beautiful summer sky. His journey had been kind to him, and his life was free from pain. He wanted to see adventure and danger, but this was not his path … not this time. The vision within my closed eyes was so vibrant and fragrant.

I said, "Your adventure, my dear child, is to cherish your life and share this goodness with the others already near you, for your danger lies within yourself. How much are you willing to risk? Give yourself away, for you will always replenish. As you give to others, you will have more and more."

He kissed me on the cheek, and I could hear the soft folding of money fall into the can … and then the gentle smile … the one that comes from the heart. I couldn't see it, but I felt it.

FEBRUARY 1 (5)
Indiana, 1960, baby Jubilee

Daddy took me to the Woolworth's counter today and held me in one arm as he ate a grilled cheese sandwich. I sensed a man sitting down beside us. I could feel my dad's back stiffen as he got up to move, mumbling something under his breath.

I didn't understand.

FEBRUARY 2
Colorado, 2009, age 49

Last night I dreamed about Mom's death. I dreamed I was at home in Indiana, and it was a hot summer day. My younger sister, Mindy, came outside to me, and I told her it felt weird looking through the living room door and not seeing Mom sitting in her chair. She asked me if I felt guilty, and I said no. There was no guilt in me at all concerning my mother. I loved my mom. I've come a long way to get to the point where I can see her kindness and goodness instead of feeling the lack of what she couldn't give me as a child. My mother had so much life she never got to live. It's not her fault she had glitches; we all have them. I think it's good when life allows us to get to know people's glitches over time. It's how we share our humanity. That's how it's been with my mother. Since her death, I sense she's experiencing some relief from what ailed her body and mind. I believe she is in a space of being comfortable in her soul—it's in this space where she and I are the closest we have ever been. She is in my heart now.

FEBRUARY 3 (6)
New Mexico, 2016, age 56

"You are Heyoka," the voice in my dream said. I looked, and there I was, dressed in stripes and a funny hat.

I said, "I'm not Heyoka!"

Then they said, "See, we told you so!"

These nighttime visitations have me wondering who I really am. I woke up and looked it up. *Heyoka is a sacred clown. Is this why I seem so different from other people? How is it I didn't already know this? Who is this being talking to me in my dreams?*

Heyoka comes from the Lakota tradition. They are sacred teachers who are notorious as tricksters and contrarians.

Maybe I am Heyoka.

FEBRUARY 4

Indiana, 1967, age 7

I hear piano music coming up from the basement. I'm going down to see. Mom is sitting at the keys, playing the piano! I had no idea she could do that!

"Mom, how do you know how to play the piano?"

"I taught myself a long time ago."

"Wow."

I just never knew my mom could do that. Why didn't anyone tell me? There is so much I don't know. I want to know my mom, but no one tells me anything.

FEBRUARY 5

Colorado, 2012, age 52

I wish there was a word I could magically say like
sorry
or
I was wrong
a word that would make love last longer
than a flower
or one particular day
or anything else that is here seemingly
then goes away
the thing about it is

you never die in me
this love
you stay there like an extra heart
beating away the days with me
maybe you know it too
maybe not
it would be enough if you smiled
and said everything would be okay
one day
and it really isn't so much about being in pain
and wanting relief
it feels more like being thirsty
like missing a friend's smile
maybe the magic word is
you were right
I'm bad
guilty
can't be forgiven
but that doesn't feel right either
I believe in magic
that my love will build a bridge
while I'm busy not looking
so that one day we can walk
between these hearts
and be friends again

FEBRUARY 6

Connecticut, 1991, age 31

Today, I learned that my brother Daniel's son, Danny, died in his sleep. He was just eighteen years old. I want to go and be with him and my family, but Jerry says I can't go. He says my brothers and sisters will taint our work and try to persuade me to give up my devotion to God. That this is a cosmic trap of evil forces trying to tear me away from my mission here. My heart struggles between being obedient and being present for my loved ones. This conflict is ripping my heart apart. I pray to the only God I know to help me and to help my family. I'll be the only one not there.

Looking at the cold road from this lonely house, I'm lost in grief for my brother, my siblings, and my children.

FEBRUARY 7

New Mexico, 2014, age 54

For as long as I can remember, I've used other people to measure and determine my decisions until I feel like I am nothing more than a shadow of myself. I'm such a coward. If only I had the confidence to listen and not doubt my own guidance. What am I so afraid of? Why can't I trust myself?

Watching others and doing what they did, obeying out of fear, wanting to please … that's how I survived my childhood. I count heavily on others to help me discern who and what is good. I've made some bad choices, and I'm afraid I'll do it again. If I hurt one more person, I feel like I would die. I'm not sure how to get out from underneath this.

Jubilee tip: Take small, slow steps toward who you want to be.

FEBRUARY 8

Indiana, 1971, age 11

Dad likes to put his hands on my body whenever he gets the chance. I think it comforts him, but I don't really know, and I don't care. I'm so used to my dad touching my butt that it hardly bothers me anymore … so long as he's in a good mood. If he isn't, he will likely hit me or anyone else that might get in his way. Butt-touching isn't nearly as bad as getting hit.

FEBRUARY 9

Indiana, 1967, age 7

My Aunt Onah is the best ever. Every day she walks to her job at the AFNB bank by the Oakley Sales, where my dad works. She walks faster than anyone I have ever seen. I like to run beside her or sometimes backward in front of her while she is on her way. Sometimes, I even follow her home, and she gets me a Pepsi. She is my very favorite, and I love her. She makes me feel as though I can be something good one day. If she can walk to work every single day, I can, too, if I need to.

FEBRUARY 10

Indiana, 1965, age 5

It is so cold outside that my brothers and sister watch for the school bus from the living room window. They do that when it is too cold to wait outside. I have my coat on, and I'm waiting for my dad to take me to my aunt Lottie's house. She watches me while everyone else is in school or at work. My dad still needs to tie my shoes. My mom is sick and has to go away again, so I don't get to see her very much. Aunt Lottie is my mom's sister, and she likes to look at the Sears catalog, but I only want to play. She says if I slide down the staircase banister one more time, she will use the paddle on me. The paddle hangs on the wall, so I won't forget about it. I suppose it's best I just go outside and wait for Aunt Onah to come home. She lives next door, and she's really nice to me. Sometimes, the cold isn't the worst part.

FEBRUARY 11

California, 2004, age 44

Hardly knowing how or why I exist
Every precious thing I've given
In trade for knowing myself
I am sick with love

I have nowhere to go and nothing to do
I am beside myself in anguish
Indifferent to hot and cold
The well invites me; the land seduces me
My heart engulfs me
Only my lover knows who I am

FEBRUARY 12

Colorado, 2009, age 49

My mother is on my mind. As a young child, I incessantly saw the possibility of her death. Her frequent trips to the asylum and physical ailments were an ever-present reminder of her frailty. I remember my brother Daniel gathering all the siblings to prepare us for the possibility of Mother's dying. I was so scared. It seems as if she's been dying all my life, and now that she's really gone, I can hardly believe it.

I keep thinking about the unfinished quilt she started so many years ago. If there really is a life review when one dies, I suppose that would have been one of her regrets. My mother was like that ... simple and pure in so many ways. I know she really wanted to finish that wedding ring quilt.

FEBRUARY 13

South Carolina, 2011, age 51

I'm here visiting Hannah, and my daughter Simone is here too. Simone and I slept in Hannah's bed last night. Early this morning, before light, I awoke to see something that most eyes cannot see. I saw smoke rising off Simone while she slept. It reminded me of a Harry Potter movie and the scene about the Dementors. As I watched the smoke pour off my lovely daughter, I thought she might be a phoenix, like me, smoldering and ready to be reborn. **Jubilee tip: Don't burn up completely before coming back to life.**

FEBRUARY 14

Kansas, 2021, age 61

This is a day for my heart ... the one that beats in another vessel. It is the day for the one who knows the corners of my mouth and can reach them with her eyes. Shhh, don't say too much, or the spell may break, and a million planets and stars will come to their ruin. For today, may all that is sacred stay so.

FEBRUARY 15

Indiana, 1976, age 16

Mom just told me she never really wanted to have a bunch of kids. She said that when God told her she would be the mother of many children, she cried for a week. Mom really wanted to go to college and be a business major. As she told me this, I saw a sad, faraway look in her eyes. I suppose when God speaks to you like that, there is no escaping the inevitability of it all. I wonder, though. Something inside me tells me she could have had what she truly wanted if Dad had also wanted it for her. I think they must have made a deal. He gets sex, and she gets to live.
Jubilee tip: Sometimes God sounds just like a man who wants you to stay in the kitchen.

FEBRUARY 16

Colorado, 2020, age 60

There is a haunting inside me. As hard as I try, it follows me around like a ghost. It blows a shadow over me, telling me a tale that I am wounded, bleeding, and tainted by my past. It is a ghoulish troublemaker warning me of my fragile state. Only prayer and fire can extinguish this pest.

"Oh, Great Spirit, come to my embers and kneel with me. Let us stop for this moment and be. No matter what else has transpired or will come, let us abide with mercy in this moment and be without condemnation or injury. Amen."
Jubilee tip: You're never alone.

Winter

FEBRUARY 17

California, 2010, age 50

Reclaiming my spiritual life has been nearly impossible. After being tormented by my mother's sick God, my dad's biblically justified violence and sexual abuse, and then a cult leader's fucked-up manipulative religious audacity, I am now taking the time to decide for myself who and what I believe is true.

Even with all that I've been through, there is still a longing for prayer within me to commune with a Divine Other. The mythology and stories from religious texts are meaningful, but my guide and rule come from within, from what I observe in nature, and from those whom I trust. It is hard to know the truth of these matters, but I'm sure of one thing: no longer will I sacrifice my life for an idea of God brought to me by a man.

Jubilee tip: God is not a man, and no man is a God.

FEBRUARY 18

New Mexico, 2014, age 54

Oh, Holy One, I ask that You show me unseen things ... that You let me in behind the veil where You are. Reveal to me the hidden layers and the mysteries. Teach me your hidden ways. If You so choose, allow my eyes to see You in all things ... allow me to sense Your presence in all situations ... show me Your ways, so I may walk with You. My gift to You is my essence, my life's breath ... my spirit.

FEBRUARY 19

Indiana, 2004, age 44

A week ago I had a dream about an Indigenous warrior. He was lying on a table that appeared to be a gurney, and my sister Jill was showing me that he was killed by a wound to his side. White curtains hung all around him, creating a secluded space. My sister was dressed in a white ceremonial gown and was a spiritual advisor to me. Outside the closed curtains, she knelt in prayer for the warrior. I knelt behind her to pray. Suddenly, the warrior came out from behind the curtains. Pulling them apart, he shouted, "I'm alive, I'm alive … look at my hair!" He pointed to his head with both hands as we watched in amazement. The dream ended.

I consulted with a Navajo friend, and he explained that in the context of the history of scalping, a Native American who still had his hair was indeed alive. A Native's hair is also widely considered the channel for receiving guidance from benevolent spirits and ancestors.

This morning I was awakened by a presence beside me. The clock read 4:09. Standing next to my bed was the very same Native warrior from my dream. He leaned over the bed to get a closer look at me. My heart beat wildly, but I wasn't afraid. I felt as though I already knew him. At first, I wondered if my eyes were playing tricks on me, so I focused on the clock, the wall, and the bed; all was as it should be. Still, he stood gazing at me. I turned to look directly at him to see if I could communicate with him. As I returned his gaze, he seemed surprised I could see him. He stood upright and vaporized. The dissipation into the air was fantastic.

Recently, I've been working on my family's genealogy. I was told by my dad that his grandmother was an Indian. I feel strongly that this native warrior spirit may be one of my ancestors.

FEBRUARY 20

Hawaii, 2005, age 45

I had an incredible dream.

I was lying on a bed of clean, white sheets with the most beautiful woman I'd ever laid eyes upon. We knew so little about each other, yet our attraction for one another was palpable. Our eyes met and locked in a deeply felt knowing. Something in my body took over, and all my senses fell in line. My heart, soul, and intimate places sounded off in a chorus of feelings I could barely contain.

She gazed into me and said, "I see you."

I looked at her in awe, and I wondered, which parts of me did she see? I asked, "You do?"

She whispered, "Yes, I do. I see a warrior, a beautiful native man," and then she asked me, "What is your name?"

I answered, "I don't know. I've lost it along the way."

She sighed, "You ... You're beautiful."

"What is your name?" I asked.

She said to me sweetly, "I am Grace."

With her hands gently cupping my face, she peered into my eyes with an intense tenderness. She pressed her soft lips to mine and pulled me close to her warm, naked breasts. Such strength surged into my being, and I knew there was no other place I wanted to be but with her.

We made love with such passion that as I awakened, I asked in disbelief, "How could this have been a dream?"

FEBRUARY 21

California, 2004, age 44

I'm staying with my brother Jesse and his wife. They are truly amazing, opening their home up to me so I can get a new start on life. Jesse is letting me drive his old truck, and I love it. The old Ford has three different metal tones from parts replaced by other vehicles. It runs great because Jesse is a kick-ass mechanic.

Since leaving Connecticut, I've been trying to see what it's like to live a free life. I met someone online today. Her name is Dee, and she seems good to me. She's beautiful, an excellent writer, and she has a wonderful sensitivity about her. We haven't met in person yet, but I'm looking forward to that.

There is a longing to live growing in me now, and I really want to believe that all the bad is behind me. I've kissed the ground so many times in gratitude for my freedom. Now I have the choice to be anything. It is such a beautiful gift to be alive and moving freely in the world—I can hardly believe it. Even with so much possibility of good ahead of me, I still feel a shadow of sadness and fear. Sometimes I think Jerry might try to come after me or have me killed.

Jubilee tip: Freedom is an inside job.

FEBRUARY 22

Colorado, 2009, age 49

Last night I dreamed I was a man making love to a beautiful woman with a spiraling tattoo of flowers cascading down her back and across her hips. I held her in my arms, and I gazed at the flowers flowing down the back of her beautiful body. Her hips were incredible.

She spoke to me that she was apprehensive about our being together that way. I listened to her words, and I could tell she was afraid, so I held her and waited for her to tell me what she wanted. She lay lightly upon me and looked into my eyes. Then we continued making love to each other. It was a consensual, intoxicating, and wonderfully fulfilling dream.

FEBRUARY 23

California, 2005, age 45

Today I met my online date, Dee, for the first time. We met at a Mexican restaurant in Ocean Beach in San Diego, not far from where I've been living with my brother Jesse. We both ordered tacos; I had a Corona, and she had an iced tea. The moment I laid my eyes on her and saw her beautiful smile, I felt as if I had known her before and we were being reunited. She's stunning.

After lunch, we walked the Ocean Beach pier, and I don't remember what we talked about ... all I could think about was her breasts. She was wearing a tailored and ironed white shirt, unbuttoned just enough so I could see a hint of a black lace bra underneath. I was mesmerized.

When it was time to say goodbye, she said she liked my truck.

The last girl I dated told me she wouldn't ride in it, and I thought that was pretty petty of her. I like Dee so much, but I want to go slowly. It is so hard to know how to live a normal life after having been in a cult for fourteen years. I feel like I'm having to learn to walk again.

Jubilee tip: Stay in the first three gears until you've got a reason to go fast.

FEBRUARY 24

Hawaii, 2004, age 44

I'm on the island of Oahu spending time with the Hawaiian Spiritualist who helped me break free from Jerry. I call her the Kahuna woman. Each day I am here I feel like a stranger in a foreign land. The Kahuna, in whose house I am a guest, looks at me and sees the sins of the white man. I've seen that look before when I used to go to the black church with Hannah and Molly. I remember a visiting pastor singling me out from the pulpit during his sermon and, in an emotional outpouring, blaming me for the atrocities against all the black folk. I didn't know what to do, so I just sat there and took it. I just recently learned that my great-grandmother was a Native American indigenous woman, but I haven't had a chance to understand what that might mean to me. So many people of color have been displaced and mistreated by white people that I don't blame them for seeing the color of my skin and being reminded of what was done to them. For the record, I am not white; I am brown. I just happen to be white-passing.

Tomorrow, the Kahuna is hosting a gathering in support of Louis Farrakhan. I'm certain I will not be welcome, so I'll go for a run. I'm very grateful to her for helping me leave Jerry, but I'll be glad when I can leave here and begin my new life.

FEBRUARY 25

Colorado, 2007, age 47

It is so beautiful here. The expansive sky and the rolling hills of the Bijou Basin lead my eyes to the majestic vision of Pike's Peak. This scene is so alive; I have never experienced anything quite like it. As the clouds roll in and the sun paints them with color, it truly is extraordinary. When the wind picks up, it excites the horses, and they race and play in the pasture. I find this scene to be food for my soul. Dee and I both love this rapture. We are so incredibly blessed.

FEBRUARY 26

Indiana, 1964, age 4

I love it when my dad comes home from work at lunchtime. My favorite thing to do is hide behind the curtains in the living room and be very still until he finds me. The first thing he does after he kisses my mom is ask her where I am. I can hear her from the other room say, "I don't know, Dad, I think you better go find her." I get more and more excited as Dad looks in two or three different places before he grabs the curtain where I am hiding. I squeal loudly, and he tickles me and then sets me on his greasy work shoe. I grab his leg as he step-swings me into the dining room. It's the best time ever. I love my dad so much.

Jubilee tip: One man can be many people.

FEBRUARY 27

Colorado, 2009, age 49

I feel that I am a failure. I told my therapist that I failed at love. She disagreed, saying I hadn't failed but just had a rough go of it. She made it sound like all my stupid choices were because of my stupid childhood. I'm pretty sure she's right. But knowing this doesn't change anything.

First, I divorced Granger. Then, I gave fourteen years of dutiful service to that psychopath Jerry. During it all, I failed my children.

And now, Dee. We're really struggling, and she started drinking again. I've tried so hard to salvage this one. I feel utterly defeated.

FEBRUARY 28

Colorado, 2009, age 49

Dee and I are still legally married, but we are presently separated. It has been torturous to watch her leave behind thirteen years of sobriety over our split-up. I'm trying in every way I know how to help her, but there only seems like so much I can do.

This afternoon, Dee called me from a motel phone.

"Jubilee, I need your help. I can't find the truck. I think Donna took off with it, and now I'm stranded. Can you come and get me?"

"Where are you?" I asked.

"I'm at the Broadway Motel in Denver, Room 22."

"Okay, stay here, and I'll come and get you. I'm an hour away."

The Broadway Motel has a reputation for high drug traffic and prostitution. I did not know this, so I approached it like any other motel. I knocked on Room 22, but no one answered. I looked around, but the only person I saw was a janitor vacuuming in a vacant room.

He saw me looking around and said one word, "Korean?"

I said, "Yes."

Just like the janitor, Dee is also of Korean descent. He pointed to Room 24 with a nod, and I knew she was in there. I was a little concerned at this point that the janitor would have felt the need to be watching out for her. I knocked on the door, and a black man in a muscle shirt and jeans, holding a drink, answered.

"Hi, I'm looking for Dee," I said.

He sized me up and said, "Come on in."

The door closed behind me, and I instantly felt vulnerable. I saw another woman in the back of the room with Dee's shirt on, and then I saw Dee … she was sitting on a stool, in her bra and blue jeans, and she had a look in her eyes that told me she was high on a drug.

I said to her, "Where's your shirt?"—knowing full well where it was.

That other woman came forward and gave Dee back her shirt, saying she was just having some fun. While I helped Dee put her shirt back on, the man came toward me and started to shove me to the back of the room.

"You need a drink," he said, and upon saying this, he hit me square in the right nipple with his index finger. I was stunned at how much the strike of one finger could hurt. The pain shot through my chest, and I began to pray.

Now I knew this man meant me harm.

All I could think to say was, "I'm five years sober."

He became excited, turned, and gave me a big high-five as though I had just said some magical incantation. I took this moment of grace as an opportunity and grabbed Dee by the hand.

"We have to go now …," I said, pulling her out of the room. I was so scared at that point I didn't dare look back.

After sobering up, Dee told me they were holding her in that room because they had planned to pimp her out for sex. I had gotten her out just in time. That really scared the shit out of me, and I'm so glad we both got out of there.

MARCH 1

New Mexico, 2022, age 62

What do I know about crypto? Absolutely nothing, and yet here I am invested in something that systematically hijacks my nervous system. It takes great effort to keep myself from falling into this trap. I may make a lot of money from this game token, but it is nothing I have worked for or deserve unless the endless hours of staring into my phone count for something. The chance at millions is hypnotic and nerve-racking. I am only human, and that amount of money would change my life … I think. Meanwhile, what am I doing to earn an income and work toward financial independence? Think about that one, Jubilee.

One thing I have noticed about this group of people is that they all want the money badly. So much so that they are willing to endure and justify countless false promises and endless bad behavior just to turn around and feed more money into an abyss with nothing to show for it. At first, I saw it as something fun to do with friends and felt it was worth the low investment risk. Now, I am worried there may be loss of life if this thing ends up being a scam. Some people are in deep financial trouble, and they just keep investing more. I nearly believe there is a demonic influence involved.

Jubilee tip: If it seems too good to be true, it probably is.

MARCH 2

Indiana, 1971, age 11

I'm going to ride my bike to see my friend Aymee. Her dad is the doctor in town, and we're friends. She lives in a big, fancy house and has the coolest stuff I've ever seen. I always wonder what it must feel like to be her. She likes me because I taught her how to throw a football. She's three years younger than me, so I make sure I tell her things I think are important. The other day we were under the old bridge, and someone had painted some bad words under there.

"Aymee, do you know what that word is?"

"No."

"That is 'Fuck.' I don't know what it means, but it's a bad word. You need to know about it because people use it a lot."

"Thanks."

"You bet."

Jubilee tip: Always look out for your buddy.

MARCH 3

Colorado, 2019, age 59

Some weird shit happens to people who own my artwork. Not everyone experiences crazy phenomena, but more than a few have. One pencil portrait I did for a friend of mine was in a house fire.

The wall where my drawing was hanging was black and charred except for the area around my drawing. It remained untouched by the flames. Then, there was the time I sold a watercolor portrait of Mother Teresa to an acquaintance of mine. She instantly became enamored with me, moved to the town where I lived, and began inserting herself into my private life so much so that I had to break friendship with her. Ten years later, out of the blue, she contacted me and demanded a large sum of money for the safe return of my painting or else she would burn it. She ransomed Mother Teresa! I did not pay the amount, and I have no idea if the blessed saint made it through the flames.

Over and over, once someone has bought my work, we've become estranged. Three times, it happened with dear friends of mine. One time was with a lover. Coincidence? It doesn't feel like it. If that weren't enough, I have foretold deaths in my drawings and accurately depicted past events I had no previous knowledge of.

I went to my medicine women to see if they could shed any light on this mystery. They said that my work carries strong energy, and some people can't accept how possessing my work challenges them. It is like they have to grow to coexist with my work. If they don't, then things happen that will drive a wedge between me and those who are guardians of my work.

My paintings should come with a disclaimer:

Be advised! This art is alive and will fuck with you. If at any time you feel you are no longer compatible, please seek to sell and/or rehome this piece.

MARCH 4

Colorado, 2021, age 61

One of the ways in which I have used my spooky gift of seeing pictures for others is by creating what I call Energy Imprint Drawings (EID). I've already done many of these over the last fifteen years, and there are still several people who would like to have one, but it almost seems as though I'm breaking some kind of cosmic rule.

Winter

When I look into that space in my mind's eye and search for a unique image connected to my subject, some of the pictures that have come to me have been premonitions of deaths and past events I couldn't have otherwise possibly known. It used to seem like a harmless parlor trick, but now I'm not so sure. I just don't feel like it's my place to get that personal with someone I don't know, and with all the other strange phenomena that have followed my work, I think it is safer for others if I stop.

I don't want to be casual with another's life in any way. I'm not going to do these drawings anymore.

MARCH 5

Connecticut, 1999, age 39

There are so many rules I obey. Jerry trusts my faith more now, and I have more privileges and permissions to connect with my loved ones. I can send my children gifts and write to them any time I like. Sometimes I make phone calls too, but I have to avoid abusing his trust or causing any alarm. The most important thing is that I am obedient.

It's terribly lonely, but I feel much more connected to God and my family when I'm actively taking care of myself. The more I embrace and understand this caring for self, the more I feel like a real person. I've been working out more, drinking less alcohol … I've also been writing—secretly. I am always being watched, so I have to write in code, but I know what each word means. I've even allowed myself the freedom to reevaluate my understanding of God. All of these things are helping me become more of who I really am.

During my studies, I've come to believe that God and love should be synonymous. Violence, hate, and bigotry are qualities I don't believe God favors, and yet somehow by the Christian definition of God I've been taught, He contains both love and violence, both kindness and cruelty. This one thought has given Jerry license to do whatever he wants because as the scripture says: *To the pure all things are pure.* And yet he chastises me for thinking any of his actions can be bad. Anything he does is good—because he is God's chosen. I guess that means he can abuse our cat and lie to people about money.

There are still so many contradictions in this faith that I am trying to come to terms with. For instance, I'm looking deeper into my love for women and how I feel about homosexuality. I don't dare talk with Jerry about it because he's already told me he considers it an abomination (as does God). Still, I have found another answer that makes more sense. After all, I am a person, and God is an idea primarily defined by men. Who is God to me? What do I believe is true for me? I just don't buy into a man telling me what I can and can't do with my body and then shaming me if I don't fall in line. Especially when the standard of his own life is held up to a different measure.

Jubilee tip: Patriarchy is never a good idea.

MARCH 6
New Mexico, 2014, age 54

Turning
no eyes save my own
people pry
cats stare
love meanders
dogs yearn
My well drinks of itself alone
Purging this bodily earth
redeeming water's burst into cool stillness
slake my thirst
I dip
seeking reflection
I drink
and know my own alone

MARCH 7 (7)
Indiana, 1965, age 5

I don't understand what I'm seeing on the TV. Police officers are trampling and hitting black men in business suits and dress coats. Are these men so bad that the police need to beat them? I asked my mom, but she just stared at me. I'm afraid to ask my dad because he hates black people. My mom just said, "They want to vote." Then she went back to rocking and staring.

MARCH 8
Indiana, 1964, age 4

My mom is so big and so sad. She has a baby inside of her. I wish she felt better.

MARCH 9
Indiana, 1964, age 4

My little brother was born today, and I can hardly wait to meet him. His name is Sam Elan, and I'm so excited to have a little brother. Now there are nine of us. My mommy is tired, so I will help everyone and let her rest. I hope they will let me hold baby Sammy. I'm very strong.

MARCH 10
Oregon, 2021, age 61

… and then Abra said, "… there is a fine line between despair and determination."

I feel these words playing over and again in me, and I know I possess both. She's so young to know such wise words. There are times when she says something like this, and it may very well be a conceptual idea she is having, but when I hear them, I know I have lived them. I have felt that paper-thin line between despair and determination. It isn't to say she hasn't experienced them … she must have some knowledge of it or she would not have known to say it to me in the moment I needed to hear it.

MARCH 11

New Mexico, 2013, age 53

My closet is full, and every so often, that shirt appears … chartreuse and gold.

Thoughts of the dance, the night you and I were laughing.

You loved me then, so I wore it.

It fit me then, and I've not worn it since.

Some shirts fit for only a day.

Colors fade, seams tighten and give as if to change their minds.

Love inspired me to look the way you saw me.

The mirror of you.

Today, my closet reminds me to wear my soft blue tee.

MARCH 12

Oregon, 2021, age 61

Signs of spring are starting to show. It almost feels as though a warm breeze is about to come. It's still cold, but the sun is warm. Soon the leaves will peek out of the buds, and the spring flowers will brighten my walks. I love seeing the daffodils and tulips; they are winter's miracles. The flowers will have a good run until summer begins, given no late frost. Curious how the dormant bulb can endure so much cold, yet as soon as the petals are bare, the slightest frost can take them. It is the beginning of a new cycle. Oh, how these seasons teach us there is never actually a death, only sleep.

MARCH 13

Hawaii, 2004, age 44

I'm sitting on the lanai here in Kaneohe, Oahu. There's something about the deluge of showers that makes the sweet smell of the forest more vibrant. The ʻilima flowers, red ginger, anthurium … all of these and more permeate as the music of the rain upon the metal roof creates a wild dance of sound. From my spirit, I began to sing …

Kane, cry for me, let the wind blow and wash away from me a myriad of fears.

Secret places white as snow, deceitful places forever go to the windward side and away, away. To the windward side and away, away.

Kane, cry for me, let the wind blow and wash away from me a myriad of tears.

Secret places white as snow, deceitful places forever go to the windward side and away, away ... to the windward side and away, away.

MARCH 14

Oregon, 2021, age 61

Because of the ongoing COVID-19 pandemic, I enrolled in a remote death doula course. It was something to do while being cooped up and lonely. The training has been incredibly useful, but then it got me thinking about the possibility of psychically following someone into the afterlife. This thought unnerved me, so I made an appointment to speak to my instructors privately about whether or not this was a risk for me, given my propensity for vivid non-physical experiences. I really wasn't interested in accidentally getting pulled into someone else's afterlife journey.

After I spoke with my instructors, I found out that other people have already done that kind of work. It's called being a psychopomp. A psychopomp is an escort into the afterlife. I'm pretty sure I must have a natural talent for this kind of thing.

My teachers then directed me to the author Raymond Moody, who has studied near-death experiences (NDEs) at great length. I've enjoyed reading about his findings, but the one book that has really intrigued me is called *Making Sense of Nonsense*. In this book, Moody talks about nonsense being a bridge between science and spirituality and goes on to explain how he believes it can be used as a tool to reach into the afterlife.

This exploration into nonsense is something that truly excites me, and I am going to investigate it further. Instinctively, I know this is a critical path for me to take.

MARCH 15

Kansas, 2020, age 60

There is a lot of fear in the air. We've been hearing news of a new contagious disease, and it might be dangerous. As of a few days ago, states have started to impose restrictions on businesses and social gatherings. I have no idea what this will mean for the future.

My brother's house also burned to the ground today. They lost everything; it's all ashes. In this climate of fear and uncertainty, this level of loss is hard to imagine. I made an online wedding registry for them so people could help them replace at least some of the material things they need for daily living. These are frightening times. The eerie silence of empty streets and this creeping cloud of viral assault are enough to set the hairs of any sturdy being on edge … and then pile on a personal devastation. God help us all, especially my dear brother and his wife in their hour of need.

MARCH 16

Hawaii, 2004, age 44

The air feels cool on the island tonight. The night is dark, but I know the mountains are there.

The dew has settled on a million leaves. Roosters wait to wake up the world while nestled in their beds of hay.

I came here for help, and I need to start over. A powerful and commanding woman, Kahuna, rules this house. She is a spiritual guide, a witch, a force. I am here to wipe my slate clean, and she says she can help.

This is another house with strict rules. She makes the rice and sits me down in the chair before her. I can see through the giant window at her back the forest and the mountains, and they are awesome. Her sons sit to either side of me, and their voices also speak with command and prophetic knowledge of me and my life. Like a humble supplicant, I tell her my dreams. I am scared to death of this woman. She reads scriptures and signs, and she pours her magic into my bones. I am naive. I am nothing. I try to please her. I try to please God yet again.

Even so, there is a looming chill in my bones today. I am faced with an uncertain journey. So much has been lost, and though I see the glimmer of life's light before me, a certain sadness still seeps under my skin. Grace, where are you? Take me in your arms and gather me to your breast. I need you.

MARCH 17

Colorado, 2021, age 61

There's a tiny new growth of hope in me trying to live. It's thrilling and strange and so tender and sweet. This sprig is so busy taking root in me that it devours my life in order to live. Nourishment is hard to find for this precious thing.

The audacity of this seedling! Is this trickery? Is it deceit? How dare it come and offer new life to this crone? Ah, this young shoot carefully wipes my tears. It lives to give me hope. It's a joyful baby who cares nothing about my doom and gloom. I'm so curious about the tenderness of its fresh leaves. How each day it unfolds a little more and stretches to the sun. A subtle smile comes over me now, and I want to care for it, for us. I want this life to grow. This is what happens when an older woman finds a young lover. It's exhilarating.

MARCH 18

Hawaii, 2004, age 44

I woke up in a sweat, mortified. I had a dream. I know it means something, and it terrifies me because I really don't understand what it's trying to tell me.

First, I saw a beautiful woman … one of the most beautiful women I've ever seen. Her hair was long and black, her eyes were almond-shaped, and her cheekbones high and defined. Seeing the curves of her exposed back, I came closer and gently kissed her shoulder. We lay together in a hot spring, caressing and kissing one another. We both wanted to make love, but we didn't.

I walked on and saw a door leading into a room ahead of me. It appeared to be a doctor's office, but it also looked like someone's home. I entered another room—this space felt clinical and cold. An old woman with wild, wiry gray hair stood at the head of a gurney. She was a witch doctor. I recognized her, but she didn't recognize me. She barked orders to her assistant, always calling me a "him." I felt myself becoming hypnotized. "You are a bird," she said, and then I was chirping.

Her assistant kept poking me in my side; it was aggressive and uncomfortable. I looked at her severely and told her, "Stop poking me, asshole, or I'm gonna get pissed!" But I was still chirping like a bird. Still entranced.

"Hmm, how interesting," the witch said. She snapped her fingers, and I popped out of my trance. I was confused, but then I looked into her eyes and remembered why I was there.

"You told me you could open the window for me to be free," I said to her.

With our eyes fixed on each other, she replied, "Lie down here."

Then I was on the gurney, and she was at my head. She waved her hands rapidly over the left side of my face, then to the right, then on top. I was again hypnotized, helpless in a state of trance. Then she drilled bolts into my skull to hold a steel band around my head. I felt the pressure of her bare fingers boring deep into my bones. I could see and hear everything. I was awake but paralyzed.

Then I heard a voice, calling me:

"Auntie! Auntie!"

It was Apoakelia, the Kahuna's son. He was a lovely young man who always made me feel welcome.

"Auntie!"

He was trying to save me.

Apoakelia was walking toward me through flowing white sheets. Lights were firing off inside my head. The white sheets were hanging on lines. Those lights and lines were my own synapses, out of control, full of electricity. I felt the witch's drill still pressed against the left side of my head, but now she suddenly stopped as if she was being interrupted. *Apoakelia has come for me.*

He has saved me.

Thank you, sweet soul.

As I awoke, I could still feel the holes in my head, and yet I felt saved, safe.

Jubilee tip: In your hour of need, help will come.

MARCH 19

Colorado, 2018, age 58

And then suddenly, a dangerous woman slips in through my cracked window.

Poised, she sits at my table, March winds moving through her while she sits perfectly still.

No stand of pines, no mountain pass, no wall of flames or closed door can stop her.

She moves untamed, this force of Grace.

Bringer of blades of grass and flower buds; she moves me.

Venomous as she seems

I need her ...

Hers is a royal entrance, the resurrection of ancient souls hidden too long in their dreams.

As she dances, her dress flows like the murmuration of starlings.

Her hair is the same, and all the while ... even the evergreens lose winter needles.

I, in my space, open the window wider to bring my daughter home.

It is Spring.

Spring

Reflections on Spring

SACRED EAST

Sunrise, daffodils, the force of creation, and the wind. *Oh, the wind.* Molly, as I knew her before the last frost took her too soon. My Spring was a defiant one. I only knew the ways of the elements that battered my young heart. Though I learned quickly how to run with the wind, scale the heights of trees, and dodge the flaming arrows. Spring, like a fiery sister who must always have her way, made sure I would survive. She was loyal to me that way.

That was then, but now this Season has taught me to act in her play. I see the rising sun and smell the morning dew on the grass, and something stirs me to drink this life. Birth pangs no longer dismantle me; instead, Spring emanates within me as the divine spark, and I know she has invited me to join in. Her bubbling well hasn't drowned me after all; instead, this living water fills my cup.

MARCH 20

Colorado, 2009, age 49

My granddaughter was born today. Our sweet Bella. My first daughter, Hannah, born on the winter solstice, gave birth to her daughter on the spring equinox. The synchronicity and loveliness of this make my heart smile. I really don't know what it means, but it gives me pleasure.

MARCH 21

Colorado, 2011, age 51

The mystery of life is great. When I look for something, it seems to magically appear. When I am afraid of something, it also seems to appear. It's as though there is a living consciousness that weaves into and through everything. Moments in time swirl where they were birthed and appear to go on living. Sounds leave our mouths and head toward distant planets and beyond. There seems to be nothing that isn't alive. Is this God?

MARCH 22

New Mexico, 2013, age 53

I look to the East as I begin this new day. The sun rises with my longing, and I pray:

"Oh East, spirit of the dawn and of creation … help me find myself again. May your kindness grant me grace and renew me. Guide my heart to not be troubled by life's hardships, and help me to live in love and joy. Hear my heart's song and grant me my longings and desires. My gift to you is my effort and devotion, and I will always look to you for my help."

The East replies, *"You, my mourning dove, are the light you seek. Arise and let yourself be born anew this day. Take up your challenges like arrows in your quiver and draw back the bow to meet your desires. With the precision of playful delight, you will reach them. There is nothing more tender to me than your life and your devotion. I am with you."*

Spring

MARCH 23

Connecticut, 1993, age 33

Is it right for a man to dictate God's will for my life? For my flesh? How can someone else know who I'm supposed to have sex with when I don't know? I wish I could hear from God as directly as Jerry does because then I would know for myself what is right, true, or … righteous.

Jerry tells me it's God's desire, and then he takes me. He calls me his consort. He tells me that I will wear his crown and sit by his side in the afterlife. That God has joined us as One, and the flesh is a reflection of that ordained union.

I leave my body every time.

Is this you, God? Are you the one who wants my flesh?

A feeling of sickly gray consumes me when he insists I touch him or have sex with him. He smells of sulphur, and his sweat is putrid. There is a bulbous protrusion on the left side of his penis, and I wonder why it's there. I try to love him because I love God, and this is my service to Him.

Jubilee tip: Love can never be coerced. Not even by God.

MARCH 24

Connecticut, 1991, age 31

As I reflect on the death of my best friend and a few others I have known, I can't help but wonder why death is so hard to understand and accept. I get that physical separations are traumatic and mournful … I have felt that, but on the other hand, if we knew for sure our loved ones were still alive somewhere, wouldn't it make it all easier to endure? I feel as if the way our culture experiences death seems a little lopsided. As the seasons turn, there is always life again, right? Why would our lives be any different?

I would like to do away with the fear of death and daydream more about where I will journey to next. It would be nice if this process were a little easier to accept. I think, one day science will prove life after death, and then maybe letting go and transitioning will be easier. My prayer is to gracefully move through the wheel of seasons and to pass this knowledge on to my children.

MARCH 25

Indiana, 1970, age 10

I brought water in an old Pepsi bottle and went to the edge of the cornfield. I'm on a mission to prepare for battle. The dirt here is silky smooth, and it's the best dirt to make mud.

I made perfect mud balls about four inches thick. Then, I stuck my finger in the middle of each ball to make them hollow inside. I lined them up to dry in the sun. After they were hard dry, I filled the holes with sand and tiny rocks. Then, I plugged the holes over with more mud for the last part and let them dry again.

Do you know what I just made? Dirt bombs. Nothing is better than my dirt bombs when battling my brothers in a dirt-clod war in the side yard. When I throw them, even if I miss, they explode and throw bits everywhere! Watch your eyes … it's a war out there! **Jubilee tip: Watch for flying objects.**

MARCH 26

Connecticut, 1995, age 35

Jerry invented a gun that emanates sound vibrations. It has a knob on the back where he adjusts the tonal highs and lows. I've seen him use it to help heal people by placing the gun on a bruise or sprain and manipulating the frequency. He's used it on me before on my lower back, and it seemed to help.

He said that he developed the technology while he was in the military working with Admiral Rickover and now the government is modifying the tech to deploy it as a weapon. I believe the weapon part because I get terribly sick when Jerry turns it up without anything covering the end of it. I really wish he wouldn't do that so often. When he wants to drive a point home with me or just remind me of his authority, he'll use it. I really hate it when he does that.

Spring

MARCH 27

Indiana, 1968, age 8

My dad brought my mom and my new little sister home from the hospital today. She's number ten in the family, born on the 25th. I wonder if my mom is finished having babies now. I hope so because I really don't think she should have any more. My sister Jennifer is having a baby pretty soon too. It's kind of crazy they're both having babies at the same time. My new little sister is really cute, and I love holding her. Her name is Mindy Lynn.

Mom is so tired.

Jubilee tip: Just because you can doesn't mean you should.

MARCH 28

Indiana, 1972, age 12

Oh my gosh, I just saw our cat, Greyhound, walk into our car's hubcap. I think this cat is completely blind. I mean, wow, how does he figure out how to get around outside? I hope he's going to be okay. Mindy will take care of him. She loves all the strays, and they love her.

MARCH 29

Colorado, 2011, age 51

Lorraine is in Birmingham for work, and I miss her as always. She is such a joy to me, and her love surrounds me with such warmth of comfort. Despite my mistakes in getting to this point, it was worth every stumbling blunder I made. She and I fit, and that fit is something I would never jeopardize, trade, or give away. I hope she feels the same way.

MARCH 30

New Mexico, 2017, Age 57

Last night I couldn't sleep, which is strange for me. I am afraid I'm not attracting goodness into my life. Somehow, I've lost track

of what it means to be a good person. My habits, my daily efforts ...
it's all meaningless to me.

"Do you think I'm a good person?" I asked my wife.

"Yes," she said, laconically.

"How do you know?" I asked.

She said that the animals all love me and that she just knew it. I'm
glad she thinks I'm good, but something still feels off inside me.
What am I really doing that helps another person? I just know there
is something more for my life ... something more I have to give.

MARCH 31

Connecticut, 1991, age 31

My entire life I've struggled with strep throat so much that I just
had my tonsils removed. Granger is out of town on business again,
so I'm staying with my best friend, Patty, from church, and her
husband and two kids. She lives in a big house, but there's an apartment upstairs, and our teacher, Jerry, and his family live there. She
is helping to take care of me and watching Hannah and Molly while
I recover. I really appreciate what she is doing for me. My throat is
killing me, and I have zero energy. Thank God I have help.

Patty and I are very close, so she tells me pretty much everything.
Since I came here to recover, she has been telling me that Jerry is
saying I should leave Granger ... to not go home. I'm shocked that
he would ask this of me because Granger is my husband and the
thought of leaving him has never entered my mind. I'm scared. I
don't know what to do. I need to talk to Jerry myself.

APRIL 1

New Mexico, 2017, age 57

It's been over a year since my accident with Dr. Brown, and I'm
still not able to work. Recently, my daughter Simone and her family
sold their home and uprooted their lives to come and help me. I
am one of the owners of Prickly Pear Café, and Simone signed up

to work for us while I recover. Today she came home from work crying. It's not the first time. She doesn't feel treated as an equal at Prickly Pear, which challenges her and saddens me. The other workers seem to think she's a snitch because she's the owner's daughter. I'm sure there's more to the story, but the bottom line is that she's miserable. Even my friend and business partner, Tory, is making life harder on her.

I've come to know this town and this land, and if it wants you, staying is easy and seamless, but if this is not the place for you, it will spit you out or kill you. I've seen it happen with others, and I don't want my daughter and her family to get stuck here in Tell the Truth or Else. I feel the need to change something. We need to move, and it needs to happen soon. It's time to get her out of this place. I'm afraid her life has been nothing but hell here.

APRIL 2

Connecticut, 1991, age 31

Since recovering from my tonsillectomy at my friend Patty's house, I've been sleeping on her couch. Since Jerry insisted I didn't return home, Granger now has taken custody of the children. I am alone here with my church friends, and I am at the mercy of Granger to see my daughters. This is not my home, and these are not my people, but I believe Jerry hears from God and that this is where I am supposed to be.

Early this morning, before light, I awoke to a horrific vision. Lying above me on the back of the sofa was a figure. It was fleshy, bulbous—hideous. It stretched the length of the couch, sneering at me. I was terrified. Even though I tried to scream, all I could do was whisper a screech. I felt like my vocal cords had been severed; no one in the house could hear me.

There were demon cherubs flying directly above my head. Their laugh was sinister as they flew around my face. They were tormenting and frightening me. The fleshy monster lay on the couch and watched the show. I grabbed my head and buried it into my pillow as I prayed for God to save me. What horrible madness was this? Does this beast live in this house? Am I crazy? *Dear God, please help me.*

Jubilee tip: Demons are real.

APRIL 3

Connecticut, 1993, age 33

Dear God ... if only I could see my children again, I might come back to life. Do you see me, God? How much more must I do to prove my devotion to you? I have given everything to you. There is nothing I love that I have not sacrificed at your altar. Take my life now, please ... this pain is more than I can bear.

APRIL 4 (8)

Indiana, 1968, age 8

Something feels bad, and I want to know what's going on. The television news said Martin Luther King, Jr., has been killed. He is the preacher I saw before on the news. I see people fighting and crying. This is so bad. Mom is in bed, but Dad is watching the news on TV. He's not saying anything to me. I asked him why men were carrying signs that said "I Am A Man." He just said, "Never you mind."

He never talks to me. He only talks to Mom. But Mom doesn't look at anything on TV unless it's one of her daytime shows or the evangelist. After Dad went into their bedroom, I could hear him saying, "They're all hoodlums" and "They have to be stopped." I couldn't hear what Mother was saying back to him. I really don't know why my dad thinks black people are bad. Something inside me hurts.

APRIL 5

Connecticut, 1991, age 31

Things have changed so suddenly—Granger and I have split. He took the children by force, and there is nothing but the feeling of death within me. I'm here with my friend, Patty, still sleeping on her couch. Jerry and his family are upstairs. I shouldn't feel so alone, but I do. I left Granger, and there is nothing I can do except rely upon his mercy to see the children. Jerry keeps telling me my sacrifice will be rewarded and that I am doing the right thing. I trust him, but I am dying inside without my girls. He tells me I am saving their lives. I don't understand, but I trust Jerry knows God's will for me.

APRIL 6

South Carolina, 2019, age 59

I spent the most amazing week with Hannah and her family in South Carolina. It's a joy to have this time with them. Something completely unexpected happened to me today. As Hannah and I talked, she began to tell me about her husband, Brian, and the blessing his love is to her. She said he lays his hand upon her head and speaks words from God. Listening to Hannah, I thought about how the Divine voice of the Great Spirit speaks to us and through us for others. I asked her if it would be okay if I had him give me a blessing, and she said it would be just fine.

Brian agreed, and soon we were sitting together as he began:

"I have seen your struggles and your pain. I know life has been difficult for you. I long for you to come to me and lay down your burden. Let it go. Let go of the fears and the heartaches you carry. You can share so much love, joy, and wisdom with your children and your grandchildren. You have a gift. Your gift is your ability to make others feel better when they are with you, but you must let your hurts go. Take comfort in those who love you and enjoy this life. You will be here for a long time, so run now; be free and live."

Just when I thought the Great Spirit was busy watching out for everyone but me, my son-in-law channeled a voice that felt true and good … a god I could take comfort in. Thank you, Brian, and Great Spirit.

Jubilee tip: The sins of your past are not always passed down.

APRIL 7

Oregon 2021, age 61

"Jubilee, you know the rules: stay alive, don't eat poop, and get yourself home,"

Abra said this to me as I was about to make another cross-country trek back to Kansas. The way I come and go is dizzying, and yet she seems to understand this is what I need to do.

"I'll come back as soon as I can."

APRIL 8

Connecticut, 1976, age 16

Since I turned sixteen, my dad said I could date boys ... that is, any boy except Granger. My dad doesn't like him because he has long hair, smokes, and lives in a trailer. Since trying to see Granger has made my life a lot harder, I'm dating other boys. In all honesty, I've been kissing boys since I was fourteen.

Something I've noticed about kissing is that mostly boys are gross and have no idea how to kiss a girl. Since this is obviously important, I decided to make a list.

Here's what I have so far:

> "The Green Light." – I really like you.
> "The Peck." – I like you but not that much.
> "The Saint Bernard." – You might need a bib for this.
> "The Truffle." – I'm listening to you as you are listening to me, and I can hardly wait to know more of you.

So far, Granger is the only Truffle I've kissed.

APRIL 9

Indiana, 1977, age 17

Mom is pacing the kitchen, and her eyes are wild with her voices. She hovers near me, and the hairs on my arms start to stand up. *Just don't, Mom, please, not now.*

"You're going to hell tonight," she said. She repeated, "You're going to hell tonight."

She paused and said again, "God told me you're going to hell tonight." Her eyes were vacant yet possessed. She wasn't there. Something else was.

I was pretty sure I was already IN hell, but I asked her callously, "Mom, do you know what time God is coming? I have a date, so I want to make sure I'm not out when He decides to come."

She didn't hear a word I said.

"God told me, you're going to hell tonight, you're going to hell tonight, God told me."

"Thanks, Mom. I'll try and be ready."

Jubilee tip: You don't always need to listen to your mother.

APRIL 10

Colorado, 2019, age 59

My medicine circle is where I speak to the four directions, the above and below, and all that lies between. Each direction is set with a large rock that has volunteered to go on this journey with me. Between each of these large stones are smaller ones and branches too. At the East, there is also a key. This is private, so I won't share this.

This place is set up among the tall pines and the large rocks. As I look to the south valley, I see the majesty of Pike's Peak. I have a guardian who also abides with me on this land. He is a Native warrior, and I know he walks with me here. Each day when I go to pray, I pick up a rock from the land and whisper my prayer into it. Then, I lay it beside my last prayer. These rocks that have prayed with me form a large circle. Many prayers have been said here. The circle keeps growing.

Yesterday, a large tree fell between my medicine circle and my stone circle of prayers—such precision in its placement. Mother Tree stood nearby and heard her voice speak gently:

"Look here, child, what a cutting divide between petition and practice. Do you see? Connect your walk and song. Believe in the hawk's flight and the raven's caw. Do this, and you will find your sanctuary."

61

APRIL 11

New Mexico, 2017, age 57

Today, we confront the reality of a dog being himself. During the night our dog, Trouble, diligently dug a tunnel under the fence to allow our young chickens and ducks a path into his pen. He's a bird dog. Birds are important to Trouble. Specifically, catching, killing, and eating them.

Suffice it to say, we are almost out of birds.

My three-year-old granddaughter, who has never seen death up close and personal, doesn't understand how Maui the duck was alive yesterday and today ... he is cold and lifeless. How do we save Maui? How do we bring him back? Where did he go? I wonder if she'll remember her first death experience as vividly as I do.

She is devastated because she loved those chickens and ducks, and she's trying to understand what the spirit world is. I suppose this will be the first of many death lessons for her. As for me, those lessons get harder and harder to understand, and I've come to realize The Great Mystery is called that for a reason. Welcome to Earth, sweet granddaughter; we are all looking for this answer.

Jubilee tip: Don't ask your bird dog to guard your chickens.

APRIL 12

Colorado, 2009, age 49

I told Lorraine today that it felt as though something inside me was dying. She seemed to think that it was something that needed to die. There were words I was not saying to her. I felt like a horrible person for the way we both left our previous relationships and the depression in me was turning into a sickness.

The part in me that needs to die is the lies.

APRIL 13

Indiana, 1966, age 6

Vacation Bible School is one of my most favorite times ever. This week, we got to watch a super good artist paint a picture of Jesus on black velvet while he told us the story of when he walked on water. We also got to make a necklace out of macaroni noodles and build a house out of popsicle sticks. Then there were cookies and Kool-Aid. I never get to have those kinds of snacks at home, so that was sooo good. Then we got to play outside. The biggest thing we did all week was practice our special song to sing in front of all the church adults on Sunday. All of us kids stood up in the front of the church and did special hand motions that went with the song. It's called "I'm in the Lord's Army," and it goes like this:

I may never march in the infantry *(march in place)*
Ride in the cavalry *(pretend to ride a horse)*
Shoot the artillery *(aim and fire a pretend gun)*
I may never fly o'er the enemy *(arms like a bird)*
But I'm in the Lord's army! *(salute)*
I'm in the Lord's army! *(salute)*
I'm in the Lord's army! *(salute)*
Vacation Bible School was the coolest ever.

APRIL 14

Indiana, 1973, age 13

My Grandma Heartwise recently died. I've never seen a dead person before, and it was pretty weird. I mean, she looked like she was asleep, but it was the kind of sleep that doesn't breathe. Her skin was hugging her bones too. I was glad they put soft pillows in there since she was going to have to be in that box for a long time. I hope that made my mother happier. At Grandma's funeral, I stood next to my mom. She cried. I didn't feel anything and just stood there wondering what all the fuss was about since to me she was a cruel and mean person. I figured she was gone now, and that was that. I asked my mom why she was crying, and she said she loved her mother and now she was gone to heaven. Heaven seems like a pretty good place, but they better watch out for Grandma ... she ain't too nice.

The Tell

APRIL 15

Colorado 2009, Age 49

I wrote this story on parchment, and after I read it to Lorraine, I tore it down the middle and gave her half and I kept half. Is she the answer to my desire? I don't know.

~

Once upon a time, long ago and far behind, the Earth said to the Sky, "Let us create together." The Sky agreed, and a union was made at dawn, and from it sprang forth two daughters. The Earth had made a child in its likeness and was delighted. Likewise, the Sky was exhilarated because her daughter was so much like her. The children of the Earth and Sky loved each other and played together in fields of green and skies of blue ... they each had a part of the other within them. They were kindred spirits in love with life and enraptured one with the other. So strong and dedicated was their love for each other that the Earth and Sky thought to test their love.

The Earth said to the Sky, "Let us take our children and place them in different times and places to see if their undying love for each other will bring them back together." So, they gathered up their children and sent them off. The daughter of Earth was shot like a swift arrow, as far across the land as possible. The daughter of Sky circled through the air and sailed on the winds to the farthest reaches. Never had they been placed so far from the other. How else could the test of true love be measured?

Then the parents watched as the unfolding of time, events, and pure undying love took place. At once, the call of desire entered the realm of the ether. The child of Earth cried out, and the daughter of Sky returned the call—neither one hearing the cry of the other ... save with the heart. Through countless ages and lives, they sought and tested love to see if the voice of the other could be found. Journey after journey, and finally, when it seemed that not even love could conquer the abyss, the dreams began.

The daughter of Earth dreamed of her treasure, and the daughter of the Sky dreamed of her love. The daughters walked hand in hand through the passages of time and the change of seasons. They walked by water and sky, mountains and sunsets. They came to each other in dreams and found each other's hearts. They created children together, and they worked side by side. They became each other until a new universe was born of Earth and Sky, grace and peace.

And then they awoke ... their hearts were broken to see that it was only a dream. They walked on, clinging to their desires. They walked on while the sun set and the wind blew. Each forlorn over dreams unfulfilled. And still, they walked on.

Then came a day like the others before; the Sky and Earth looked on ... the children, now old, full of desire, enough to hold fast to hope, came to a crossroads where they met. At first, they did not recognize each other, but as they spoke, the embers of past longings began to appear.

"Do you remember me?"

"Yes, I remember you."

"... and do you love me still?"

"Yes, I love you still."

APRIL 16

Colorado, 2024, age 64

"Never play editor and author at the same time."

Abra just said this to me as we are working on editing this book together. I have so much respect for her literary knowledge. But more than that, she is wonderful, and I love her.

APRIL 17

New Mexico, 2013, age 53

I am in Estancia, New Mexico, at Grandmother Flor de Mayo's 40 Acres, where all thirteen indigenous Grandmothers have come together to consecrate the sacred Seed Temple. The ceremony is a celebration of the seeds needed to begin a new world, if it should ever come to that. The Grandmothers are here to bless the Seed Temple, and I am here to watch and partake in this sacred event. The ravens are flying closely overhead as the Grandmothers watch, wave, and laugh. I have a close affinity with ravens—partly because they are the animals of my indigenous astrological sign, but especially because they came to me to help me leave Jerry and the cult.

The temple is a collection of seeds and seed balls kept as emergency rations in case of global catastrophe. The stairs to the vault descend about ten feet underground, and in the vault, the shelves are stocked high with jars and jars, displaying all the colors of life. The seeds come in reds, yellows, and browns of all shades. A kaleidoscope of hope.

I saw large bins containing seed balls, and each bin had images drawn on top of them. The images showed men, women, and children along with the number of seed balls that would keep them alive. The pictures were drawn so that anyone of any language could understand the instructions. This vault is a chamber of life, shrouded with a shadow of doom. It awaits the world's end, as we know it.

I hope this will never be needed, but it's nice to know it is there. **Jubilee tip: Expect the best but prepare for the worst.**

APRIL 18 (9)

Connecticut, 1997, age 38

Jerry just sat at the table across from me and told me a story. He told me about how today is the anniversary of when his friends died in Beirut.

"I was in the Army, stationed in Beirut. They blew up my buddies, my best friends—among so many others. It should have been me, but I got called offsite to report to my commanding officer. As soon as I left, bombs hit our barracks."

"You could have been killed?" I asked.

His face was expressionless. "It wasn't my time," he replied. He stared me down and continued, "And no one can take me off this planet but me. When I go, the world will know it. Life will not remain the same. In so many ways, I am holding things back that will otherwise bring ruin to this world. Mark my words."

I sat and looked at Jerry in wonderment. I was afraid of him.

Spring

APRIL 19

Colorado, 2009, age 49

I am sitting with Lorraine's partner, Linda, at her kitchen table having coffee and banana bread. Linda used to be a journalist, so she's always good for interesting conversations. She has a pensive look on her face like she's searching for words. I've been visiting their log cabin house for several days. It's a beautiful getaway.

"Do you mind if I ask you a question about leaving the cult?" Linda asked.

"Ask me, and I'll let you know, but it may take me a while to get through the cult files," I chuckled. "I still get pretty anxious about it."

"That's okay, I have time if you do. When did you know that the leader wasn't what he presented himself to be, and how did you finally get out?"

"Yeah well, it was a process, really. It didn't happen all at once, although I did have a pivotal experience that finally brought me to say enough."

"What was that?" she asked.

"I'll never forget it … after nearly fourteen years of devotion to this man, it was Thanksgiving of 2003, and I had just gotten a pair of jeans and a jean jacket; Jerry's wife, Tamra, bought them for me. The jacket was cute—it had lots of snaps and a mandarin collar. I tried it on for Jerry a few weeks before Thanksgiving. Emphatically, he said he didn't like it. He seemed to think that I was dressing like a boy. I didn't wear it again after that, but I also didn't really think too much about it. Well, what happened was on Thanksgiving Day, and we were getting set to have our church members come over for Thanksgiving dinner. It was early, and I let the dog out to pee, but it was chilly outside, so I grabbed the jean jacket and put it on. Jerry saw me with it on and immediately became super angry. He took it as a full-frontal assault on him, as though I was defying his authority in my life. He would also get the same way if I put my hair up into a bun. He was convinced I was always striving to be more masculine, and he hated that."

"Wow, what an asshole. Really? He had that level of control over your life?"

"Oh, he had all the control, but it got way worse. After seeing me in the jacket, Jerry got angrier and angrier. By the time the other church members arrived, he was nearly stroking out. One of our church members asked me what I did this time, and I shook my head in dismay. Jerry was spouting off about me being a disrespectful ingrate who would never amount to anything and that if I made *Dad* mad, there would be hell to pay. Of course, *Dad* was God, and Jerry was the golden child."

"No way. I would have left at that moment."

"Right, I suppose I should have, but nothing seemed that easy back then. Jerry was abusive, degrading, and threatening, but he still held authority over me. He certainly didn't spare any words in front of the others as they came in for Thanksgiving dinner. It was tragic theater, and I was nearly always the scapegoat."

"What did you do?"

"Well, this particular awakening hit me at that moment: I am forty-four years old, with no friends aside from a few monitored relationships within our small congregation. I had no life; I didn't even have a choice about what I wore. It was the most pathetic life anyone could have. I felt like I was dying, and I had to get out. That was my big awakening that day."

"So, after the whole Thanksgiving Day freak-out about your jacket ... is that when you knew you had to leave?"

"It was when I knew something had to be done, but I also knew I couldn't do it alone."

"Do you mind if I ask how you got out?"

"No, it's okay. I had a lot of help though. One of the secret ways I kept from going crazy was through the internet. It was an AOL dial-up, and I think it saved my life. I would get a drink and go into my room. It was really my office, and although I never slept there,

I had a futon, a desk, and an internet connection. It was where I had the most freedom because I could get away with closing my door. When Jerry retired upstairs or was busy with something else, I would go online into a lesbian chat room called the Pink Sofa and talk to strangers."

"I'm so glad you had a way to talk to other people. That must have been a real lifeline for you."

"Yeah, it really was. The internet was new then, so I hardly knew what I was doing, but I'm so glad I found that site. I met a few interesting girls. I started talking to one of the girls in the room a lot. Her screen name was Kiss."

"Nice handle."

"I thought so too. Kiss and I talked quite a bit over a few weeks, and I started to really like her. At first, I couldn't bring myself to tell her the complete truth about my situation. I mean, it was all kind of too much, and I was interested in maintaining a friendship at the very least, so I left out the part about Jerry and the house of his followers. I focused instead on the things I had learned, like my art and my religious studies. She thought that was fascinating, and it gave us something to talk about besides what was really going on with me. We were getting more intimate in the chatroom; then my real issues started to surface. Finally, I told her how desperate I was to escape the prison I was in. Then came the words that I didn't want to hear. Kiss said, 'I have a teacher who can help you.'"

Linda's eyes widened.

"Yikes!," she replied.

"Right," I said. "I told her, uh, no thanks. I already have a teacher who has held me hostage for fourteen years. I'm really not looking for another one. But she said, please believe me. This teacher can help you. I said no. Several times. But gradually, I was so desperate for help I was ready to try anything."

"Were you really scared?"

"I was so scared, Linda. I had sacrificed everything in my life that meant anything to me. After making so many sacrifices to prove my devotion, trying to walk away from it somehow meant that it was all a giant mistake and that I gave my life for nothing. This was a really difficult thing to admit. It still hurts my heart so much."

"I really can't imagine, Jubilee. I'm so sorry."

"Thanks, Linda, but I need to stop now. We can talk more tomorrow if you still want to hear the rest of it."

"Absolutely."

APRIL 20

California, 2005, age 45

I dreamed of a faraway land. Pyramids … a goddess …

I called her name. *Isis!* Then I heard my mother's voice say, *"Jubilee, don't give up."* Instantly, I saw an image that Isis had given me. It was a raven perched upon her shoulder, spreading its wings, preparing to take to the air and fly away. I could hear the familiar tone of Isis's voice inside my head, saying, *"All you have to do is spread your wings, Jubilee, and we will carry you."* And then I saw what I had seen so many times before … the wind and sky and the earth … embracing me in their loving and mighty arms. The wind dried my tears, and the sky made the promise to carry me upon the wings of her love. The earth held me in her embrace and offered me a foundation to walk upon.

Jubilee tip: Jump, and you'll grow wings.

APRIL 21

Indiana, 1971, age 11

There's no one to throw the ball with, so I throw it to myself. I have an old catcher's mitt and a hardball that belongs to one of my brothers, so I throw the ball up as high as I can and then catch it. Sometimes I catch it behind my back, and other times I catch it with my hand down by my side. I like doing tricks with it. I love anything I can do with a ball, but it's better when I have someone to throw with. I'm getting pretty good at it because I do it a lot. Sometimes if I misjudge the catch behind my back, it hits me in the head. It hurts for a while, but I just keep on going. It's how you get good at something; you gotta work through the pain.

I wish I could get out of this house.

APRIL 22

California, 1980, age 20

After trying to get through college and failing twice, I ended up living with my art teacher, Ms. G. Ms. G had the idea of me meeting an old student of hers, so I went out, and we hung out together. This girl told me she was a lesbian and had just broken up with her girlfriend. She was pretty distraught and just so happened to have a bottle of 151 rum in the car. As the night progressed, she was doing donuts in the schoolyard with her car, and I was in the passenger seat white-knuckling it. Before I left her that night, she leaned over into my seat and kissed me. I had never been kissed by a girl before, and it nearly sent me through the roof. So many feelings woke up inside of me that it scared me to death. I left as fast as I could get out of there.

APRIL 23

Colorado, 2009, age 49

During morning coffee, I decided to dive back in. Linda was sitting with her hands wrapped around her coffee cup and still in her house robe.

"So, here I was in Connecticut talking to this new teacher in Oahu that my friend Kiss connected me with. She tells me to get a brand new Thompson Chain Reference Bible and a bunch of grape juice, of all things. Every day I started by opening that Bible up wherever it would land, and then from the top left page to the bottom right of the opposing page, I was to read my message for that day. She called it my Allelo."

"So, this was your new teacher?" Linda asked.

"Yeah. I call her the Kahuna lady. I had to wash myself with grape juice morning and night while reciting the Lord's Prayer aloud in the shower. Morning and night, morning and night. She had me record all my dreams too. I had to write the messages that came to me. But hold on ... the *very* first thing I had to do was send her money, whatever I could afford. It wasn't much, and I think she thought I had more money than I did, but I sent what I could because she was helping me get out of hell. She wanted more money offerings soon after that, so I had to keep scraping up enough to appease the gods without letting Jerry know what I was doing."

"Uh wow, how did you feel about that? It sounds a little shady to me."

"It seemed that way sometimes, but you gotta remember, I was desperate. So, I would put the cash in a white envelope labeled 'Offering.' I then put the offering envelope into an envelope addressed to her home on the Island. Each time I sent her money, I was banking on the Kahuna lady or the mountain gods having some real power that could find me a way out. It didn't matter who ... I just needed out.

"There were a few more rituals she had me do. I had to piss on a tissue and place it in a white envelope along with another piece of paper with the names of those I wanted to escape from written down—I wrote every cult member's name on that paper to be burned along with my pee, just to be safe."

"No way. What the hell ..."

"Yeah ... and I am still, to this day, dumbfounded by why I had to piss on it. I burned the thing while clapping my hands and speaking loudly the names of those I had written down inside that envelope."

Linda laughed, "Oh my god, Jubilee!"

"You should have seen me in front of the gas grill, two and a half stories up overlooking the parking lot because it was the only safe place where I could burn the damn thing. It felt crazy; I was on the balcony doing the sacred Hawaiian pee ceremony."

"This is so crazy ... I really am sorry you had to go through that."

"Thanks, I appreciate that. I wanted so much to scream the names and get them the hell out of my psyche, but I couldn't risk getting caught, so I had to do it quietly in front of the grill—I was in full view of the neighbors, and I didn't want anyone in the house to hear me. I mean, really, what could I have possibly said to explain what I was doing?

"While I was busy doing all these rituals, she said she had some kind of sacred council working on loosening the bonds so that I could break the chains that tied me to Jerry. So, I kept doing it just the way she said ... scriptures, writing, grape juice, The Lord's Prayer, pee, clap, and burn."

"For fucks sake ... I'm sorry for laughing."

"Not a problem. I laugh at it, too, because I can't cry enough to feel better about it."

"You want to stop now? Let's have a drink."

"Yeah, for sure."

APRIL 24

California, 2005, age 45

Today, Dee and I are getting married, and I feel like a princess in a fairytale. Although I was married before, I didn't have a dress or anything special. Today, I have an elegant dress, great hair, and professional make-up, and, well, everything is perfect. Somehow, I don't think I will ever be as beautiful as I am today. My brother Jesse has come to walk me down the aisle, and Dee's son is walking her down the aisle. The setting is so breathtakingly beautiful here at our friends' gorgeous home in Laguna Beach. The house sits on the edge of the cliffs overlooking the ocean, and it is more than I could have ever dreamed of. These two beautiful men are hosting our entire ceremony. They are so incredibly generous.

This wedding has been difficult for some of my family members because I am marrying a woman. Most of my family are not here with me today because they believe love and marriage between two women is wrong. The two who have come to celebrate with us are Jesse and Barbara and my two sweet daughters, Simone and Hannah. I know Molly is here in spirit as well. I will forever be grateful to Barbara and Jesse, who came to honor me today.

I am in love. This is who I want to spend my life with; today, this is what matters to me.

APRIL 25

Colorado, 2009, age 49

It's after lunch, and Linda is ready to keep talking. She started this time ...

"Did any of these rituals make your situation any better?"

"Yeah, actually, I think they did. You have to know that after doing all of these rituals plus the money I sent, I was all in. Then, an interesting thing happened. I had this dream where a big magic sword severed a cord between Jerry and me—after that dream, I seemed to become stronger, braver, and a little closer to leaving. So, yes, I believe it did make a difference. It's hard to describe what happened, but something shifted. Before that, I was completely bound to Jerry. It was as though he owned me. Whatever he said, I did. He controlled my every move. Even my feeble attempts to have outside friendships in secret would never work out. As soon as he found out, he ended that connection. The threats, ridiculing, and warnings ... especially his threats to withhold his special protection for my family and me. He was frightening and dangerous."

"He would threaten your family?"

"Yeah, he would metaphysically hold them hostage every chance he got. If something terrible happened to someone I love, Jerry would explain how he had saved them from a worse outcome. Sometimes he would threaten to remove his protection, leaving them open to the natural cruelties of the world. I remember when my sister Barbara hit a deer, and it came crashing through her windshield, kicking her and causing her to lose control of her car. It nearly killed her. Jerry and I had recently argued, and he declared he was withdrawing his grace from my family. Right after he stripped away his grace, my sister almost died in this accident. I was devastated, and he warned me yet again that the well-being of my family was in my obedient hands … and he said it just like that."

"Mother 'efing Bastard, what the fuck!"

"Yeah, Jerry delivered threats and warnings regularly, but with the big Kahuna and Hawaiian sacred council on my side, I felt a window of opportunity opening.

"I started to make a plan. The next thing the Kahuna lady instructed me to do was to get help, so I called my family. 'I need to get out of here' was all I had to say, and soon, there was an entire network of people from around the world praying for me and planning my escape. What followed was a covert plan to get me out. My stress levels were off the charts. I believed if Jerry found me out, he would no doubt kill me or torture my family.

"Jerry had many fear tactics. One of his favorites was to go on and on about how much he utterly hated his mother. He said that the only thing he couldn't understand about his father was why he never killed her."

"No fucking way."

"Uhh, yes. There were so many hate stories about Jerry's mom, and I'm pretty sure he told them all to me. When he really wanted to scare me into submission, he would say how much I reminded him of his mother. Those steel gray-blue eyes were cold as ice. On those nights, I slept with my hands close to my neck, and I would get as far as I could from him. That was tricky since I slept on the floor next to the couch where he slept."

"So, you slept on the floor next to him for all those years?"

"Yeah, I did. I really, really did."

"Well shit, Jubilee."

"It was all I knew, Linda. And I just thought if I did everything he said, just like he said it … maybe he'd let me see my kids and family. He manipulated the fuck out of me."

"I see."

Linda's face reflected disbelief and possibly a concern that I was mentally ill. I've seen that look before … it's the way I looked at my mother when the voices were at her. I kept on with the story anyway.

"I had to do everything secretly. I got a small storage bin nearby and started gathering up a few things to take with me. One of the only things I was still allowed to do was send gifts to my family and kids, oh, and make coffee runs. So, I would put my own stuff in little boxes, address them like I was going to mail them, and sneak out through the cellar with a few things at a time and put it all in the car. I'd sneak back in and then make a coffee run for everyone. I would go as fast as I could to take the boxes to the storage unit and then grab the coffee, all in the time it would typically take me to just go and get coffee. My heart raced wildly. I was afraid of burning in Hell. The guilt was insane, and all the time I worried I was making a mistake. But now I had a new mission. I was saving my own life and my daughter's life and maybe the lives of those stuck in that house and in that cult. Kiss, the Kahuna lady, and now my family had my back—and my family was planning my rescue. I had to stay strong and on track.

"As Jerry's wife and daughter, Tamra and Jordan, and I were driving one day, I said to them both, 'If I have to leave, it's not because of you, okay?'

"I looked at Jordan in the rearview mirror. Her eyes were misty and solemn.

"'Please know that it is not because of you, okay?'

"'Okay.'

"Tamra said, 'You better not leave me here alone with that man.'

"'I don't want to, but I may have to.'

"That is as much as I could say to Tamra and Jordan. I genuinely loved them, and I knew I would miss them. I would do whatever

I could to help them. I lied, though. I wanted more than anything to leave, but I really didn't want to leave those two—that hurt. The only consolation was that I showed them how to walk away, should it come to that for them. Can we stop now?"

"Yes, of course."

APRIL 26

Colorado, 2007, age 47

I'm sitting in the DIA terminal next to my gate, waiting for my 1:15 p.m. flight to take me to Atlanta and then to Charleston. My youngest daughter is getting married this weekend, and I'm excited. Several of my siblings will be there, and they're also hosting a shower for her on Friday. I can't help but wonder what that's like because only two of my nine siblings attended my wedding to Dee. There was no acknowledgement of it being a legitimate ceremony, and so, although I am glad for their support of my daughter, I also feel pretty shitty at the same time. I'm trying hard not to think about it.

My sweet girl is thrilled about her special day and so psyched about being married. I really hope things work out for them and they'll be happy together. They're both so young with so much of life to live ahead of them, yet we never really know what lies ahead. We never know anything other than what is happening in the moment ... and then it's gone, and then it's gone, and then it's gone. Elusive time that can never be harnessed. Never. My advice is to ride it and know it will lead into a myriad of other waves—and if we are lucky, it will be the best ride ever. My ride has been pretty good lately, even with the drama of my marriage. Whatever comes, I'm grateful and will continue to ride these moments, embracing all that I find good. I hope Simone will do the same thing and, above all else, stay the beautiful person she is.

Jubilee tip: The map is not the journey.

APRIL 27

New Mexico, 2014, age 54

In the early morning, I awoke to see between the veils. On occasion, this ability comes to me. It's a gateway into the unseen world between waking and sleep. Today, something nudged me to wakefulness. Before me was the most intriguing scene. A tall, dark figure with a long, feathered headdress stood in my bedroom doorway. Just behind the dark figure stood an entity made entirely of light. In the tall figure's right hand, he held a rattle that seemed to be made of maize. He alternately shook the rattle twice vertically and then again twice horizontally. Repeatedly, he did this. As I sat in bed watching this fantastic scene, a cosmos with planets and stars swirled around the bedroom above me. Lorraine was lying asleep beside me, and as much as I wanted to wake her to see this beautiful event, I didn't want to miss any of it. Soon, the vision began to fade into the dim light of our room, and I laid back down in awe of what had just happened. I don't know who those beings were, but I felt as though I was in an important ceremony.
Jubilee tip: Open your heart to the extraordinary.

APRIL 28

Colorado, 2009, age 49

Linda started to inquire more about the cult after breakfast.

"I know we've been talking about this for a few days now, but honestly, I'm fascinated. Are you still up for it?"

"It's fine. When I talk about it, I am also processing it, so I feel like it's good for me in a way."

Linda smiled and went on, "I can tell it was hard for you to leave Tamra and Jordan. What was your relationship like with them?"

"Tamra and I were comrades. We each had our cross to bear with Jerry, although she worked nights and slept all day, so she missed all the main events that I went through with him. He treated her like a queen but whispered to me that she would die soon due to her recurring cancer. She was also the breadwinner. Over the years, I realized that he had to protect her as a resource. I don't know if he loved her or not.

"One of my jobs was to protect Jordan. I might as well have been her bodyguard because she was never allowed out of the house alone, not even to the yard or driveway. I always had to keep my eyes on her. Jerry told me I was protecting Jordan from being kidnapped. He had this idea that federal agents were after his military secrets, and if they ever got their hands on Jordan, they would blackmail him. My job was to keep her safe. So, I did."

"Are you fucking kidding me? What was wrong with this guy?"

"I wish I were kidding, and looking back, I have no idea what was wrong with him …. But in a way, watching Jordan helped me cope with being separated from my children, and I never really believed anyone was going to kidnap her. Jerry was so paranoid. He left TVs on in every room all day …"

Linda laughed. "In case the house was bugged?"

"Yeah, exactly, it drove me nuts."

"Eventually though, I wanted Jordan to see me leave … that way she would know it could be done."

"Jesus, this is horrible."

"Yeah, well. There were times when I felt so guilty for leaving. I had been there for close to fourteen years at that point. They were the only family I had. Jerry was a pretty bad man, but his kindnesses blinded me to his true nature. He comforted me. His was the only intimate touch I had for years, and he knew it. I genuinely believed he was the best man I had ever known. What I didn't realize in those moments was that Jerry was the one dictating God's will to me, and it was never God at all."

Linda paused. "It's really hard to believe you thought he was a good man."

"I was raised to endure bad behavior and to accept it as normal. I got it from both of my parents. My dad was a brute, but everyone thought he was a hero. He was a fire chief … he saved lives. He was a deacon in the church. In the case of my mother, it was her illness. I feel like I was trained to be with a man like Jerry.

"One day I was having doubts about leaving when I cried out to the universe, *'God, all the gods, anyone who can hear me, please let me know if I am doing the right thing!*

"'I need a sign.'

"I was standing in the kitchen, two and a half stories up. Outside the windows, there was a giant oak tree, and the limbs stretched almost to the windows. As I stood there asking for a cosmic hand, two enormous ravens flew down and perched on the branch in front of me."

"Had you seen them there before?" Linda asked.

"No. And I had never seen any black birds so big before, not ever. They stared at me through the window. I took them as my sign that what I had begun and was about to do was the right thing. Later, I found out that Ravens are my Native totem, and I'm sure they were there to help me."

"That's pretty cool."

"I thought so too. So, about a week before leaving the house, Jerry started grilling me about what I was up to, but I wouldn't tell him anything. He was afraid I was going and pulled out all his tricks, but nothing would work with me anymore. He tried to act wounded by dropping to the floor and feigning a heart attack, but I had seen that performance before. Then he acted loving and tried to seduce me, then he got mad, and finally he started to threaten me.

"I had taken to sleeping on the futon in my office room, and he would pound on the ceiling, trying to get me to come to my regular bed on the floor. My floor bed was a piece of rolled-up foam Tamra brought from the nursing home where she worked. She called it an egg crate. I would lay it down with a few blankets and sleep on the floor next to the couch where he slept. Each morning, I rolled it up and placed it in the closet. Every night, I would lay it down to sleep."

Spring

"So, you slept next to him on the floor all those years. Was he dangerous? Did he hurt you?"

"Yes, he hurt me. And he terrorized me, but he never left a mark ... well, except for that one time he gave me a black eye, but he said that was 'an accident.' The moment he squared off at me, I knew I had to stand completely still because he was about to throw a punch at me. He could throw a punch so fast and accurately that if I moved at all I risked getting hit. He warned me not to move, so if I DID MOVE and he hit me, it would be my fault. He was such an asshole. There were so many other threatening things he did to me, and then he said it was all part of my 'training.'

"On January 9, I stood looking at them for the last time. They went shopping, and I didn't go with them. They just knew I was leaving. After they left the house, all I could do was gather as much of my belongings as I could and get out before Jerry changed his mind and came back to stop me.

"I called my brothers, who were waiting for my signal nearby. I let them in, and they loaded me up and took me out. I was stricken with fear. Terrified that Jerry would hunt me like an animal. I was moving on adrenaline, so I have very little memory of those last few moments—the closing of the door, the family I would never see again, the threats that would no longer haunt me but still did and sometimes still do. I am telling you what I know is true, but honestly, in those final moments, it seems as if an angel came and picked me up and carried me off to the next place.

"I directed my brothers to the storage unit, picked up the things I had stored there, and we started our trek to Indiana. It was a long drive. I lay there next to these brave men I grew up with and tried to rest. It was nothing I could wrap my head around, and I was uncomfortable and numb. When we finally got to my brother Mark's house, I kissed the ground."

APRIL 29

Indiana, 2017, age 57

I went to see my dad in the nursing home today, but when I walked into his room, all I saw was an old and weathered shell fast asleep. Once he woke up, I could still see him inside his worn-out body. It was good to see him, but he thought I was his sister. Maybe I look a little like her now. My sisters tell me that he thinks of me and misses me at times. As odd as it feels to say so, I feel the same way about him too. I try to let myself enjoy the parts of him I believe were good.

Mostly, I think of my dad as a kind of wild animal who takes what he wants when he wants it. I think he has feelings, but remorse has never been something I have seen in him. He is a man-beast, and still, I don't want to hate him. He is my father, and he helped create me. He fed me and tied my shoes; he locked the doors at night and checked my arms for cuts when I ran through the front door glass. He also beat me and touched me in ways that he had no right to do. He threatened and scared me and stalked us girls in our bedroom while he thought we were sleeping. He called me names and made me think I was less than nothing.

I don't want to judge him lest I be judged, and I know none of us are without fault. I don't want to hate him because, in some way, I believe if I condemn him, I will be condemning myself. In my heart, I think my dad is not a very good human being, and I really don't know what to do with that.

APRIL 30

Colorado, 2018, age 58

Today, I heard screams pour from the hallway. I opened the door to see my friend who is staying with us collapsed on the floor, wailing, handing me her phone.

"Kurt! Kurt!"

I took the phone from her and held it to my ear. I heard the voice of Kurt's mother:

"He's been murdered!"

"I have to go. Kara needs me," I said as I hung up the phone.

Kara was inconsolable, and all we knew was Kurt had been beaten and left for dead. Kara's fiancé, an Indigenous man of the Mescalero tribe, was now gone.

Alcoholism and drug abuse coupled with substandard living conditions lead to violence and sometimes death. It isn't just the men who suffer. Young women disappear and are never found. Indigenous peoples are faced with these devastations, an ancestral relic of genocide. These wounds are so deep that there seems to be no healing, no reparations, no justice. This heartache is beyond repair.

This is life on the rez. We'll miss you, Kurt.

MAY 1

Colorado, 2010, age 50

Today was the first circle medicine ceremony I've ever performed; one of my medicine women showed me how. As the sun was going down, she showed me how to ask for rock volunteers for the circle. I promised them I would set them back in their places when we were done. I felt several of them volunteer as they became more attractive and animated. We set the center stones first, then the Eastern gate, and the key. The South came next, then the West, and finally the North. The ceremony began at the East gate.

"If you would be so kind, please share your wisdom and interaction with me," I asked.

"You were born here. The East is the place of your rising, your birth, and rebirth."

Then to the South ...

"What is this feeling in my belly?"

"This is the purging fire of refinement."

"I must confess I have had no love for you, South. My earthly mother has shared much heartache arising from the South, and my daughter died there. I have had hate in my heart for you.

"It is time to release this if you are willing.

"I am willing."

"Then so be it. Go in peace and think no more of this. Let the warmth and comfort of my being heal you now."

"I traveled to the West where I felt an immediate feeling of meeting an old friend. I felt as if I could pour my heart out to the presence of the West.

"Hello, old friend."

"Hello"

"I feel as if I know you."

"Yes, you do. Tell me all your woes; empty yourself here so you may be renewed. This is your time of gratitude and rejuvenation."

"Thank you. It is so good to see you again."

The North bid me come closer, so I bent down to listen.

"I am your true Mother, the spirit of your ancestors."

"I feel you. Please stay near me."

"I will; I am with you always."

I circled back to the East, and then I went to the Center, where I spoke to the Above, Below, and Middle. I had a feeling of origin and completion with the Father of my spirit. I returned to the East, and I asked permission to leave. I closed the gate with the key.

A storm was rolling in from Mother North, and the voice of thunderclouds spoke their benediction. As the sun set, I could see the crescent moon appear. The winds increased, and a raven, a hawk, and a little bird circled above us.

MAY 2

Colorado, 2008, age 48

I've been lying to myself. All this time, I've been telling myself the story that I've had no power in my relationships. The truth is that I've not wanted to take responsibility for my choices. And isn't that just fear? I've wanted everyone to make decisions for me ... even God.

Spring

When I pray, I plead with God to give me guidance, assurance … a road map. I'm so afraid of making a mistake that I would rather sit in an abusive relationship than make the decision to walk away.

I honestly don't know if this is true or not, but what if the whole reason I began seeing Lorraine was so I could be forced out of my broken marriage to Dee? Am I so afraid of confrontation that my way of finding a solution was to sabotage my relationship? I don't know. I keep thinking of reasons why I would lie like that. I'm not a scared child anymore. Why do I keep acting like one?

I didn't have the courage to tell the truth about what was really going on. Yes, my relationship with Dee was busted, but I could have said that to her face and then moved on with my life. I was afraid, so I secured my future with Lorraine, and only then I told Dee that our marriage was over. It was a really shitty thing to do, and I feel really shitty that I did it.

When I was growing up, conflict was so bad that I avoided it at all costs. I couldn't question anything without risking my life. My answer was to figure out a way to survive, and survive I did.

Even when I made my own decisions, I wanted them to be in secret. And ever since, my fear of being in some kind of danger has kept me walking in the shadow of my own life. Most people would call these secret decisions lies. I don't want to live like this anymore. I don't want to be afraid to walk in the truth of my own life.

Jubilee tip: Lies are choices that are afraid of being seen.

MAY 3

California, 2006, age 46

> *For Dee*
> Her fragrance is the salt of the ocean
> Her taste is the baker's bread
> Her song is my breath, and I sing her joy
> Her weeping, her foreverness
> In her eyes, I can see her heart

She sustains my warmth
Give me nothing more
Than what she is to me

MAY 4

Colorado, 2007, age 47

Dee and I decided to move from California to Colorado to start an animal rescue. It was her dream, and I said I felt like it was important for her to follow her heart, so we packed up and moved. Now, we have a sixty-three-acre ranch and a non-profit called Mama Bear Rescue. We're working hard to make it a success.

One of the things I've done is to bury a post out in the pasture. I call it The Listening Post, and it is about a five-minute or so walk from the house. I buried this post so I would have something to lean against while I meditated. It's a beautiful place where I can be alone with my thoughts. I can see our house, horses, pond, windmill, the Bayou Basin, and Pike's Peak off in the distance. This scene is beautiful, and it feeds me. I've spent a lot of time leaning against that post. Listening is one of the most important things I have ever learned to do. I love knowing that every bit of information ever uttered rests upon the wings of the air. Once I get past the sound of the hum in my ears, I feel like I can hear God.

MAY 5

Minnesota, 1985, age 25

My husband and I live in Minnesota with our two little girls, Hannah and Molly. My best friend from childhood called me recently, and we talked for a long time. She's living in Wisconsin on a dairy farm with her husband and two young kids. She told me she had just made some cinnamon rolls and she would stick a few in the freezer for me.

Granger's work brought us here for a year, but we are getting ready to move back to Rhode Island. We plan to see her on our way back.

We had a great talk as she told me all about her life, all the good things and some of the challenges. She and I go way back, and I love her as one of my dearest friends. I can hardly wait to see her again.

MAY 6

South Carolina, 2008, age 48

I had a perfect moment with my grandson at my daughter's wedding.

He was the ringbearer, but right before the ceremony, he had a meltdown. He's only three years old.

He tore off his little suit in the corner of the bridesmaid's dressing room and cried terribly. He was hysterical for about half an hour. We all tried to console him, but finally, his father got down on his level and spoke to him privately. Whatever he said, it calmed him down. Daddy helped his son put his suit back on, and there he was, a whimpering mess of a little boy trying his best to pull himself together. I handed the little man some pretzel snacks and let him take my hand and walk me into the ceremony. It was perfect. We were perfect. I could not have asked for a better gift. I love that precious boy.

MAY 7

Connecticut, 1996, age 36

Jerry sat there watching me tie my shoes.

"Stop," he said.

"What?" I asked.

"Don't tie your shoes like that. They will always come undone if you tie them like that."

"They don't seem to," I said.

"Do it this way." And he showed me his special, perfect way to tie shoelaces.

Jerry is religious about every bit of my life. From tying my shoes, driving the car, what to eat and not to eat, how I dress, and who my friends are. I feel so stupid. Did I never learn how to do anything the right way?

Jubilee tip: Jesus wore sandals for a reason.

MAY 8

California, 2005, age 45

This depression is bigger than I am. I feel as though I'm hanging in a black abyss, vast and cold …. I don't know if I will be okay. It feels like death.

I can't cry. Others speak, but I can't understand them, and speaking amounts to nothing. I just want the worst to be behind me. I just want to live like a normal person.

I tell my wife that I love her, but my eyes are empty. My dreams hold clues that I don't understand, and I feel so unbearably alone. I am left here, hanging. I hang so still that no one sees me, not even God.

Jubilee tip: Go outside, take off your shoes, feel the grass, and sit in the sun for a while.

MAY 9

Minnesota, 1985, age 25

My dad just called to tell me the worst news I've ever heard. His words might as well have been a telephone pole shoved through my chest. I didn't know, but my best friend was actually calling to say goodbye to me. She killed herself. It must have been just after we talked. *Why didn't she tell me?* She's gone now. I can't believe this happened. She is gone forever, and now I can't hear my thoughts. *Why didn't she tell me?*

How am I supposed to hold this? She's good! She's my friend. Don't one fucking person tell me she is in hell! I've witnessed people judge suicide harshly, more so than any other type of death. To say God condemns those who take their own lives, throwing them into the worst hell for all eternity. I can't even imagine someone saying this to her kids. I just want to find her again and help her. I wish she would have let me help her. My heart is broken.

Jubilee tip: If you or anyone you know is suffering with suicidal thoughts, please dial the suicide and crisis hotline and speak to someone: dial 988

MAY 10

Colorado, 2009, age 49

The East Gate is the womb I pass through, and I am born here repeatedly. The rising sun is my breath, and the blood that flows in me is my ancestors. They grant me knowledge so that I may learn wisdom, and my gift in return is gratitude and love.

The song we sing pierces through veils of time and space, and it is the song of a journey—a melody soaring on the wings of the raven, hawk, and the little bird.

I am tethered lightly to this planet. I've danced with devils and slept with angels, and I have slept with devils and danced with angels.

I am resting on the soft air of my mother's breasts while cradled in the arms of a good life. This says it for me today. This Mother's Day.

MAY 11

California, 2004, age 44

My girlfriend, Dee, has taught me some important things about food. They are as follows: don't eat something that is not good; delight in quality; praise and acknowledge expertise; and perhaps the one that hit me the hardest—never compromise quality when you are paying for it. She always expects to be treated a certain way and insists upon it.

One time when Dee and I, along with her son and my daughter, were visiting New York City, we decided to have dinner in

Chinatown. She ordered an extravagant dinner and one of the entrees was the duck. After she asked for Chinese hot mustard and was instead brought French's yellow mustard, she was already a bit moody. Then came the duck or should I say, the duck skin. She inquired about the rest of her duck since she had ordered an entire duck. The answer was not good.

"This is duck" was the answer.

"Excuse me?"

"This is all the duck."

Dee is a full-blooded Korean woman who knows her duck, so the battle of wills ensued.

"I want my duck." She said with emphasis.

The phrase, "This is duck," was losing its punch by then. Dee proceeded to accuse them of eating her duck in the back room while continuing to criticize their lack of authentic hot mustard. "Where is my duck?!"

We all sat and watched because there was really nothing else to do. I had never seen a public display like this before. This was my first big day in New York City, and it was all going rather badly.

When the check came, we all sat and watched Dee look at it. She left not one cent more than what our meal cost. There was no gratuity left for the staff. Our waiter took the check back to the cashier, and they both came after us as we were getting up to go. They began swearing at us and shouting in Chinese as they chased us out of the restaurant and halfway down the street. I was scared to death. Once again, Dee maintained her impeccable culinary standard.

Jubilee tip: Know when to duck and run.

MAY 12

California, 2005, age 45

No matter what I do, I keep fucking up in someone else's eyes. I'm talking about my wife right now, but there have been others too. Something stops me from being happy on my own, inside my own skin, without someone else telling me how to behave. So much about me feels broken. I want to be loved for being me and not an idea of what I should be.

All of this weighs heavily on me, and I don't know what the answer is yet. It's just been a little over a year since I was out of the cult, and in some ways, Dee reminds me of what I escaped. She is pretty controlling and keeps a close eye on me. Of course, she also has lots of great qualities, and having her as my partner has helped me ease out of a world of total control. This is just not how I want to live. I've changed so much about my life, but I don't know how to change who I am.

MAY 13

Connecticut, 1995, age 35

Granger called and asked to see me in secret. I had to create a reason to leave the house so Jerry wouldn't suspect anything. I was so nervous about seeing him again after all this time, but I couldn't say no. What could he possibly want?

I met Granger in the parking lot of the new coffee shop in Mystic. I could tell he had lost some weight, and he looked good.

"Hi," he said quietly.

"Hi, Granger, it's really good to see you."

He bought me a coffee, and then we talked in his car.

"Thank you for agreeing to see me."

"It's been a long time," I said.

He looked deeply into my eyes and said, "I need to know something."

He leaned over to me and kissed me tenderly. The old familiar feeling of his lips against mine reminded me of his passion. I could smell him, taste him, and wondered briefly if this was why he came.

"I've missed you," he said. It had been nearly two years.

"I've missed you," I said, wondering if he could see the grief in my soul. I sat with my heart racing for a moment, and then looking into Granger's blue eyes, I said, "I want to come home."

"This is why I came, Jubilee ... to see if you still loved me."

I told him, "I want to try to repair what has been broken. I want to come home to you and the girls—I can't do this anymore. I miss you all so much."

Granger went on to tell me that he had met someone, and they were talking about marriage. He said, "I still love you ... that's why I came to talk with you. I can't marry someone else without knowing if we are finished."

I pleaded, "I'm not finished ... please."

Granger lowered his head as though this was not what he expected to hear. Tears welled up in his eyes, and he said, "I'll ask the girls what they want and let you know."

He kissed me again, long and deep, and I felt our hearts beating wildly. At that moment, I thought I might get my family back, and it seemed possible that my heart might just heal. But Granger did not call to welcome me home. He called to tell me that the girls didn't want me back. He said they were afraid of going through the pain of separation again. He had decided it was best to go through with marrying his new love interest.

I've been reduced to nothing yet again. Without my girls, I am nothing. I'm finished. How can I continue to live without them? My heart has been crushed—over and over. This blow is one more strike on the broken bits of me. I am dead now, and I deserve nothing.

MAY 14

Oregon, 2021, age 61

And then Abra looked at me and said,

"Don't explain your art."

I think maybe she was asking me to not defend my art or to feel like I had to make excuses for my creations. I love the way Abra gets me to think about my personal power and how she points me in the direction of taking responsibility for my creations. My art is my voice, and everyone should have a voice. Why else are we here? Thank you, Abra.

Spring

MAY 15

Indiana, 1973, age 13

Today was really warm outside .... It's only spring, but it feels like summer. My dad has some old oil barrels in the backyard. I like to tip them on their side and balance on them so that they roll under my feet. After rolling that barrel around for about an hour, I was super sweaty, so I took off my shirt and sat up on top of the clothes-line pole. Birds like to nest inside the top crossbars, so I hung from my hands and legs and peeked inside to watch them. They're pretty cool and don't seem to mind me. Sitting up there with my shirt off, listening to the birds, felt good.

I saw my brother Daniel walking across the backyard, and he started talking to me ...

"Hey, Jube"

"Hey, Dan."

"It's pretty warm today, huh?"

"Yeah, for sure," I said.

Dan looked at me seriously as if he was about to tell me some-thing important.

"You know, I think it's time you started wearing a shirt."

I felt embarrassed. I realized he was talking about my chest.

"Oh, really? Yeah ... yeah, right ... sure, Dan."

Wow. My brothers walk around without their shirts all the time, and there's no difference that I can see. This is so dumb. I feel stupid. I didn't know I was doing something wrong. I don't even have boobs!

I got tears in my eyes, and I felt mad and kind of guilty ... I don't even know why.

MAY 16

Indiana, 1974, age 14

I don't know how this is happening, but I'm turning into a girl. I'm getting boobs like my sisters! I tried pushing them back in, but it hurt too much. This is the worst possible thing that could happen to me. I hate it. I just want them to go away. Why did God think that making me a girl was a good idea?

MAY 17

New Mexico, 2016, age 56

Prince recently died, and that's been hard for me. His death has weighed heavily on my heart this past month. I dreamed about him right after he died. The dream was so vivid. Prince was sitting naked and holding an acoustic guitar in his lap.

He looked at me and said, "They got me, but they're not going to get you."

At that moment, I felt as though he somehow saved my life. I don't always understand these dreams and visions that come to me, and to be honest, there are times I am embarrassed by them.
Jubilee tip: Don't stop dreaming.

MAY 18

Colorado, 2011, age 51

When I was on the phone with Hannah this morning, she told me there were lots of lesbians in South Carolina. She seems to think that will get me to move out there—a horde of lesbians. Even funnier, she said, "I am not sure about a choir, though, Mom. We'll have to look into that." This made me laugh! I love her so much, and I really would like to live closer to her and Simone. My daughter brings me so much joy.
Jubilee tip: Start a lesbian choir.

MAY 19 (10)

Oregon, 2020, age 60

Martin Luther King, Jr. said,
"The time is always right to do what is right."
Malcolm X said,

Spring

"Be peaceful, be courteous, obey the law, respect everyone, but if someone puts his hand on you, send him to the cemetery."

My girlfriend, Abra, said,

"MLK was to Malcolm X like the Beatles were to the Rolling Stones."

I can see that. Happy birthday, Malcolm X.

MAY 20

Indiana, 1976, age 16

Today was an unseasonably hot day. My friend from church, Johnson, came to pick me up to go hang out. He likes me way more than I like him, so I guess you could call it a date … I'm sure he would call it that. We were just driving to his house, and then I got this really sick feeling that something was wrong at home, so I asked him if he would please take me back. I told him goodbye in the driveway before I went through the back door into the kitchen.

Mom was bent over the sink. Just the way she looked made me sure something wasn't okay. At this point, I can tell from another room when Mom is *not right*. I walked behind her and headed toward my room. Before I could get to the hallway, she started talking to me, so I turned around and saw those eyes. She gets this look sometimes, and I know what it means. Supposedly, it's God talking to her, but it always feels like the Devil to me.

"God told me that you and your art teacher are doing wrong things together," she said.

I just looked at her. Here she was telling me that the one person on the planet who cared about me and my so-called life was touching me in wrong ways. The one person, Ms. G, who cared if I ate lunch, got to school on time, and took a bath … this wonderful angel in my life … how dare God speak to me this way through my mother. They were both dead wrong. Ms. G never did anything bad to me. Mom might as well have vomited in my face.

Something inside of me snapped like a brittle twig. She pointed the God gun at me and shot me one more time, but this time it was different, this time something in me died. I felt deaf. You know, like that ringing sensation in your ears after hearing a gunshot? I stood there silent for a minute that felt like an hour, and then I walked out the back door to head for the giant oak tree out behind our house. It was the only place I had to go. We kids climb it to escape for one reason or another. Today, I had every intention of climbing that oak and jumping. I figured I might as well go and finish the job Mom and God started.

The old oak tree isn't the easiest to climb. It's tricky; but what the hell, I was just going up there to die anyway. As I was on my way up the tree, I saw pieces of wood nailed to the trunk. I'm pretty sure those were supposed to be steps from an old treehouse. Old rusty nails and loose boards were hanging off the bark. I kept climbing.

Once I was high enough, the thought of plummeting to my death seemed like the wrong thing. I looked at the branches under me, and honestly, I wasn't sure it would be enough to kill me. Then an alternative came to me. I would simply beat the holy shit out of myself and see if that did anything. So, that's what I did. I bashed my head against that tree, raked my arms across the bark, and used nails and anything else I could find to cut into myself. I caused as much damage as I could. I hate God, I hate my mother, and I hate myself. I won't be anyone's victim but my own. After a couple of hours, I headed back to the house, a bloody mess. Dad was home from work by then, but I didn't care. Mom must have said something to him because they seemed to be aware of my having come back inside through that fucked-up back door. I walked back into my room like any other day. Blood was dripping from my face, and a throbbing pain in my head had begun. I lay on my bed with my back to the door as I heard my dad walking down the hall. He came into my room and sat on the edge of my bed and asked me to roll over and talk to him. One look at me answered any questions he may have had, and as he gathered me up into his shaking arms, I felt nothing. I still feel nothing.

Spring

MAY 21

Indiana, 1976, age 16

I didn't go to school today. My head is fucking killing me, and I look a mess.

God has been telling my mom stuff about me all my life, and sometimes He's right. But other times, I feel like I'm just being tormented, and no one will tell me why. Mom's spells scare the shit out of me. She tells me I'm going to Hell all the time. Morning or night in her old white slip or her dusters, and I don't know if she's taken her medicine or not. Either way, she comes after me.

Yesterday God told my mom that I was a lesbian freak who was having an affair with my angel Ms. G. I might be that girl who likes girls, I don't really know. Until a few years ago, I thought I was a boy.

It just hurts too much because I am trying so hard to be good, and this is the worst thing God could say to me right now. I mean, it's my mom saying it, but it's God saying it to her, or some fucked-up devil who wants to kill me or keep me down so I can't possibly have a chance to live a normal life … whatever that is. I'm so confused right now.

They all tell me God loves me and wants the very best for me, and then they tell me God will knock the shit out of me every so often just so I won't fucking forget that I am bad and deserve it. Oh, but don't forget that God is perfect and loves me, so he can do whatever the fuck he wants.

It's some really stupid shit.

MAY 22

Indiana, 1976, age 16

I didn't go to school today either.

The young girl in me is dead. I killed her myself instead of waiting endlessly for Mom and God to do it. I don't care what happens now.

MAY 23

Indiana, 1976, age 16

Still at home. My face is swollen and almost flat. I can barely open my eyes because of the fluid in my face. No one is acknowledging anything to me. No trips to the doctor, no cold compresses. I'm like a walking sore, and my mother won't even lift her head to look at me. Things are different here. My mom and dad seem to be avoiding me. I think they are afraid of me now.

MAY 24

Connecticut, 1991, age 31

Jerry is my teacher, and I love his words and the ways he explains the scriptures … it's like music to my ears. I've been so thirsty for this type of teaching. His southern charm is sweet. He has a relaxed authority and makes me laugh.

In private, he tells me he is a son of God and he created me to be his bride in heaven. That I am his eternal consort and will be given his crown in the afterlife. Just hearing those words made me blush. I am the one he will have at his right side? Then, he started talking about consecrating our holy union. I'm not sure what this means, but I think he means sex with me, and that doesn't feel very good to think about. I am in no way attracted to Jerry sexually.

He assured me that his wife would die soon and that his earthly marriage was not something that concerned me. He went on to say I needed to show my trust in God and that this was a test of my faith. Why would he lie to me?

I struggle to believe I'm special in any way, but he speaks with such conviction. When he looks deeply into my eyes and gently touches my arm, I feel his truthfulness. I have only known kindness and consideration from him. This is all so strange.

If I were to trust one man on this planet, it would be Jerry. I just need to have the faith to believe what he says is true.

Spring

MAY 25

Oregon, 2021, age 61

Abra and I were talking about the idea of God today. It's a lot to try and wrap my head around sometimes, and what really gets me is how people can be so certain of God's will and the rules around living. I've heard it so many times … the will of God, obeying God, trust in God. What is this God, and how do I meet him? Her? Them? Then Abra said, "There is no way to serve an entire god all at once."

Something about that sentence made me feel better. I love her.

MAY 26

New Mexico, 2012, age 52

When Lorraine and I first moved to this town, I was shocked to find out there was no coffee shop for miles. There was no way I could live in a town with no espresso. Something had to be done.

The first thing I did was to start creating a business plan. And then, as luck would have it, I met Tory, who was working at a small vitamin shop that also served lunch. She was the cook, and her food was amazing. Soon, we were chatting about my coffee shop idea, and she said she would love to go into business with Lorraine and me.

I could hardly believe it, but soon we were looking for just the right place. I was out on the street counting cars so we could determine if the traffic would support a potential storefront. One of the ideas about the coffee shop that came to me was to have all the artists in the community paint the tabletops for the café. They would all be for sale so the café could also help to support the local community of artisans. We would also use local produce and work with local coffee roasters. Everything about our café would give back to our statewide community.

We worked so hard to create this space, and today we are opening! I am so excited to have good espresso, great food, and gorgeous pastries but, even more so, to have a place where the community can gather and artists can exhibit and sell their work. I am so proud to present Prickly Pear Café!

MAY 27

Oregon, 2021, age 61

I was talking with my girlfriend, Abra, about Saint Teresa of Avila and what it meant to live a guilt-free life. For obvious reasons, I believe that guilt and forgiveness are traveling companions. I know that in all my attempts to walk a clean and integrious life, I have often fallen short and been at the mercy of another's grace and forgiveness. As we were talking, Abra said, "If being not guilty means being a saint, then we won't be forgiven until we die."

She says the most profound things at times. I suppose it's safe to say there are none of us who can claim sainthood by absolute purity ... until we die.

MAY 28 (11)

Kansas, 2020, age 60

Two days ago, I saw something I believed couldn't happen anymore.

"Mama! I can't breathe."

The world saw George Floyd pinned to a street in Powderhorn Park, Minneapolis. He died under the knee of Officer Chauvin—it was all captured on video. How many black lives must be taken? Why must we forget we are all on this planet working toward a common end? So many torturous deaths.

In my lifetime, I've known a lot of bigots. It is an opt-in disease. The blacks, the browns, Asians, and gays—our blood is the same color. Will the phoenix ever rise? Will the dream of Martin Luther King, Jr., ever be realized? God forgive us for what has happened on this planet.

Jubilee tip: Act like God is always watching because She is.

Spring

Colorado, 2018, age 58

This morning, before waking, I dreamed I was in several homes. Each one of them went up in flames. The last house was full of our animals. Each time Lorraine and I opened the door, the animals ran out and then ran back in. Finally, I grabbed our cat, Ziggy, and ran outside with him. While outside, I saw the house burning and collapsing in on itself. John Wayne was inside, and I called out to him as though he were my husband, but it was Lorraine. I looked through the flames and saw a body covered by a white sheet. It was Lorraine. I stood there holding Ziggy, waiting for her to come out, but she didn't.

MAY 30

Indiana, 1971, age 11

Today, my brother Doug tied an old inner tube to the tree in our front yard where two branches fork. I wondered what he was up to until I saw him go to the apple tree and get a bunch of little apples. He used his shirt to carry them over to the inner tube, put one in it, stretched it back as far as possible, and then shot at me. OUCH! One hit me in the leg, and I screamed. That stupid dork gave me a welt on my leg, and it hurts like crazy. He's so mean sometimes. He just laughed at me and said, "You better watch out!"

MAY 31

Arizona, 2017, age 57

I try to stay optimistic about the stupid shit that has happened in my life. I'll never know what it could have been like to have healthy parents. I'll never forgive myself for being seduced into a cult, and I'll always grieve the loss of my daughter. There are so many more things, and, yes, I am fully aware that I played a critical part in all of it, but here is my dilemma ... do I believe it could have had some divine order to it or was it all for nothing? My optimism says, *turn those scars into stars and keep doing your best, Jubilee,* but something else in me just sighs and says, *get your shit together, Jube, and stop fucking up.*

JUNE 1

Connecticut, 2003, age 43

I've studied my captor, and he has studied me. Living near this body of water, I know the mist comes in at dusk and lingers until the foghorn blares some twelve times. This life I am leading full of conflict mimics the rhythm of the tides. Ship-worn tainted waters engage with organisms ... both unnatural to the other, often taking the path of least resistance, bending the weak along the waters' course. The smell is a thick identifier. No foe is the same, and so there is no constant. Each day is another ocean, riverbed, and body requiring unique tactics. We shape in and out of position to each other's weaknesses and vulnerabilities, playing to strengths while hoping to expose the other until nothing is left but possession. All I want is my life back.

Jubilee tip: Walk away.

JUNE 2

California, 2005, age 45

Out of the breath of God, I floated
Balanced on a warm zephyr, I landed
Falling onto the bed of you, I sighed
Completely in love, I shivered
This, my countenance
Ever holy
Pneuma pulsing in my veins
Dwija
The idea that brought me to you
I will not betray

Spring

JUNE 3

Indiana, 1977, age 17

I am so tired of fighting this bad feeling. All I want is to have a peaceful emotion that's real. I need something I can count on. I need to get out of this house. Someone, please help me.
Jubilee tip: Hold on.

JUNE 4

Indiana, 1965, age 5

My sister Jill is holding me and rocking me.
"It's okay. It's all okay," she says.
I'm so scared.
"What is happening?" I cry.
"I don't know, but everything will be okay."
I'm crying so hard, and I am so afraid. Horrible screams are coming from the basement. I think it's my mother, but I don't know what's happening to her. She is in so much pain, and she is screaming. I can feel her, and no one is doing anything. My sister says everything is okay, but everything is not okay. My mother is screaming … my mother is not okay … I am not okay.

JUNE 5

Indiana, 1972, age 12

The weirdest and most amazing thing happened to me today. I was hanging from a vine in the woods near the sledding hill, and I decided to start climbing. I got part way up, and I was really trying hard. My legs were wrapped around the vine, and I clutched it tightly. I wasn't sure I could go up any farther, so I was just hanging there, in midair. Suddenly, I had the most amazing feeling I'd ever felt. My whole body tingled, my heart raced, and I felt the very best I can ever remember feeling. I can't believe what happened, and I'm not sure what to make of it, but I want to try it again and again.

When I got home, I decided to try and get that feeling back. I wrapped my shirt around both of my wrists and hung from my bedroom closet door. Crossing my ankles and pulling myself up and down … sure enough it happened again. This is so cool!

Jubilee tip: No matter what anyone tells you, orgasms are good.

JUNE 6

Rhode Island and Providence Plantations, 1989, age 29

I picked this day to have my baby. I'm twenty-nine years old, and this is my fourth pregnancy. Something about this child makes me know she had to come here. I've never felt this strongly about anything before, this feeling that I had to have this baby. I've decided to name her Simone Heartwise, after my mother, Iris Heartwise. I feel a cord binds her to me and that I will know later what it is all about. I had to choose the day she would be born because I have babies quickly and we live on the other side of the Newport bridge and our hospital is in Newport. She is perfect with her almond eyes and black hair. I love her so much, and I'm so happy she's here. I knew she had to come … I just knew it.

JUNE 7

Connecticut, 1991, age 31

Granger brought my baby to visit me today, and as I took her into my arms and walked over the threshold into the house, her sweet little voice said, "Monster." She looked afraid.

"There's no monster here, sweetheart," I said back.

Jerry came over and grabbed her leg with a little tug, and she pulled back from him with a scowl. I know this separation is hard on her. My heart breaks continuously, but I don't know what else to do. Monster? … I don't see what she sees.

Jubilee tip: Listen to your baby.

Spring

JUNE 8

Connecticut, 1998, age 38

There are times when Jerry decides to pick a victim. Tonight it was our cat, Tigger. If Tigger actually did something to offend Jerry, I wasn't in the room to see it. I walked in to see Jerry throw Tigger violently into his cage. We had a big cage for him to sleep in because Jerry's wife loved Tigger but Jerry didn't really want him in the house, so it was some kind of compromise.

"What happened?" I asked, not knowing what was going on.

"He tried to bite me, and he has to learn." Jerry was mad.

My first thought was that Jerry pretty much asked for it if Tigger really did bite him.

Regardless, Tigger was traumatized, hissing, and crouched in fear at the back of his large cage. I then watched as Jerry quickly grabbed a brick and threw it at our defenseless cat. The brick hit him with such an impact that Tigger shat himself. I went into another room and cried. I told Tamra, but neither one of us could stand up to him.

I wanted to vomit and walk out and never return, but this was God's chosen son, Jerry. How can I reconcile this? I've seen my dad beat our dog, and I've seen my brothers torture kittens, but this is horrible. This is more than I can bear.

JUNE 9

Colorado, 2006, age 46

Today, while the horses ate, I looked out over the vastness of the land and the beautiful sky. It's a stunning view, but all this beauty is lost on me. My heart hurts over the conflict in my marriage, and I am discouraged and confused. I feel empty inside.

When Dee and I first met, we had so much fun together. She was fun. She was affectionate and our sex life was amazing. We talked and shared thoughts that were deep and interesting. I really enjoyed our time together. She was so funny and smart.

Then we got married. We moved here to Colorado, and pretty soon I started feeling like she was angry all the time. She would yell at me for the dumbest things ... like how I loaded the dishwasher. Our sex life went down to nothing, and she accused me of having a dysfunction because I wanted more. Months would go by without us having sex, and for me, this was hard. What was harder still was when she would kiss me intimately, saying she wanted us to be together later that night ... all day I would be looking forward to our evening together only to be rejected when we were finally in bed. She did that a lot.

I don't understand where she went, or maybe this is the real her. I even asked her one time, "Why are you so different now?"

And she told me, "That's how relationships are ... people put on a show until they are comfortable together, and then they relax."

I thought that was pretty shitty because I have been the same person the whole time.

JUNE 10

Connecticut, 2000, age 40

Molly has been gone for nearly seven months, yet it feels like she died yesterday. When Granger called to tell me about the tombstone he and his wife placed for Molly, he never told me what he had engraved. He said if I wanted to put down my own memorial for my daughter, I could. They buried Molly in Granger's family's plot in the graveyard near his childhood home. He told me if I wanted, I could be buried there, too, when my time came.

Today was the first time I laid eyes on Molly's gravestone. I fell to my knees. I was in complete shock. There, before my eyes, was his wife's name carved into stone as Molly's mother. My name is nowhere. Anyone looking at this grave would never know I existed. How dare he? How can he possibly think this is okay? Granger must have known that I would never have the means to place a gravestone of my own—besides, who sets more than one gravestone? Why would he not acknowledge me as Molly's mother?

Spring

I am so confused by what Granger has done. Is he so interested in appeasing his wife that he would hand over my motherhood to her and dismiss me completely? Stepmother is what she was to Molly. This I get. But this, THIS, is stone. This is history that outlives generations. This is unforgivable.

JUNE 11

Indiana, 1975, age 15

A guy from church asked me out for pizza, and even though my dad said no, I waited until he went to his church board meeting and then went to ask my mom. She was in bed, as usual, and about half awake. I sat beside her and gave her the details about Dad saying no but that I thought if my brother Doug went with me, then all would be okay. She was in a fog, but she agreed. Somehow, I thought I was getting away with something because I thought her word meant something. I was wrong.

My brother went with me, and we all had a good time. While we were out, I had a bad feeling in the pit of my belly that reminded me I still had to get past Dad when I got back home. I should have known better, but I wanted what I wanted, so I took my chances.

As soon as we got back to the house, Doug hightailed it through the back door. He knew I was about to get it. Dad was back from his church meeting and stood looking at me through the back screen door. I could feel his anger from the driveway. I had committed the worst of the worst with him. Not one of my siblings has ever gotten away with defying my dad, and seeing his glaring stare through the door, I knew I wouldn't either.

He stepped out onto the porch, not saying one word, and hit me across the face with his closed fist so hard that I landed on the concrete at the bottom of the steps. I looked up at him with the same anger his fist dealt my face. I was pissed—not because of what he might do but because of who he was. He was a brute ... through and through. He used his size and strength to beat us kids up all the time, and I wasn't backing down. I'm as much a badass as he is an asshole, so I stood to fight.

I got up and walked back up those stairs … hell right, I did. As I walked by him, through the door, he kicked me in my back, knocking me to my knees. As I got up to try and walk, I felt another blow to my back … he kicked me as many times as it took for me to crawl into my room. I wonder if my mom slept through it. I hurt like hell, and I cried hard, but I don't regret what I did.

JUNE 12

Colorado, 2024, age 64

Alcohol addiction has been an adversary of mine for many years now. My battle has not been as much with my own use and abuse of the substance as it has been with my relationship with it inside of others. I do not do well with drunks or with drastic personality changes due to intoxication. Still, it has forced me to practice personal awareness and moderation.

I've learned some important things about the beast and those who fall prey to it. This cunning demigod does not build strong bridges, but rather it chains things together. The wedding, the funeral, the romantic encounter, the last and the first of most things, along with all of the in-betweens. It is so clever in its binding that the captive doesn't even know they're in bondage until the house is burning down. I think, by the very nature of the drink, it loves to set fire to things. Especially those dry and brittle things like neglect and complacency. Whoever said *the spark was gone* didn't understand this kind of fire. It tempts in such a way to say, "Here, look what I have to offer you," and then it picks your pockets clean.

This spirit is bodaciously inviting and leaps across boundaries like a pack of hounds on the hunt. It creeps into the inner chambers of depression as a best friend and confidant and then urges you to tell all your secrets to perfect strangers. There are a rare few individuals that take to the dance floor with this gent and glide with perfect grace. Having had a few dances with this partner, I know and humbly bow to this foe. I was afforded enough grace to see as I looked into his face that he was holding all of my treasures. All this time, he was whispering in my ear how gifted I was while sneaking off with my devotion.

As for those burning in this particular fire, I am so sorry, but I can't help you. I really am sorry. The most I can do is to share my journey with you. Grace be yours.

Jubilee tip: Go to a meeting. https://www.aa.org/find-aa

JUNE 13

New Mexico, 2023, age 63

Being in the tender care of an iron trap is not freedom.

JUNE 14

California, 1977, age 17

Something incredible happened to me tonight. My brother Doug and I are visiting our brother Jesse and his wife in San Diego. Doug has a friend here, and we were all three hanging out, climbing Mount Baldy, and then looking for a place to eat. As soon as the sun had set, I saw a huge glowing cross off in the distance. I begged them to follow it to see what it was. They agreed, so off we went to find it.

Once we got there, the cross was next to an old drive-in theater, now used as a church. No one seemed to be there except the janitor, so I went to the door to see if it was unlocked. To my surprise, it was open, so I walked inside the foyer. On a large table was a full-scale model of a church made of glass. I was in awe of its beauty and stood there reading the sign in front of it. Robert Schuller's Crystal Cathedral: Coming Soon!

I know about Robert Schuller from my college psychologist. He's a happy guy, and he smiles more than anyone I've ever met, except maybe my sister Jill. My psychologist used to give me sayings from him on pieces of paper to help me feel better about myself. One of my favorite sayings is, "Turn your scars into stars!" I really like that one because it feels like I have a lot of scars, especially on the inside. I also like it because stars seem so much better than scars.

This is my first time in California. It took me three days on a Greyhound bus to get here. I had to get away from Bourbonnais, Illinois. I lived with drug dealers there, and it was hard. I never knew when the police or other drug people would break through the door. We drank a lot and did even more cocaine, pot, and speed. If I'm being honest, sometimes the drugs make me feel better. It's a tough place to live, but I don't have any other place to be. Maybe I could stay here with my brother for a while longer.

I had no idea that a glowing cross would land me right here at the happy guy's church. I just needed to follow that cross. Maybe one day I will come back and sit in that glass church—by then, I hope I have more stars than scars.

JUNE 15

Connecticut, 1989, age 29

So, today my husband shot my teddy bear in the heart. He placed it on the mantle of the fireplace in our house and shot it with his .22 caliber pistol.

One of the things about being the eighth born of ten kids is that I had to go without some of the extra things other kids got to have. I never had a stuffed animal before now. A friend at church has a big collection, and she gave me this bear. His name is Thisbe, and now there's a bullet in him where his little make-believe heart should be.

When I asked Granger what the fuck? This is what he said:

"You give that goddamn bear more attention in bed than you do me. It made me mad, so I shot him."

"So, you shot the only stuffed animal I've ever had because I cuddle with it? Wow, okay, you're an asshole."

Jubilee tip: When someone shows you they're a dick, believe them ... even if it's your spouse ... especially if it's your spouse. (Revised quote from Maya Angelou)

Spring

JUNE 16

Rhode Island, 1984, age 24

There's an energy field inside my body that is constantly feeding me information. At times it just feels like noise, and other times I feel it in such a way that it speaks to me. It has been this way since I was a kid. My inner life is one giant swirling ball of information that sometimes feels like chaos and other times like order. When I feel a calming presence, it isn't so bad. I wonder if it's like how planets are made—like all the commotion could give birth to a universe in a climactic moment. I wonder if this is what my mom feels like when her voices come. It scares me.

JUNE 17

Connecticut, 2000, age 40

My strength is in stillness. I am rooted in the burden of heartbreak. It will never leave, so I am welcoming this shadow into me.

Burden, take residence until I know you as joy. Heartbreak, be mine until I know you as kin. Until the time I outweigh you with my endurance and turn you to gold.

Jubilee tip: Turn your scars into stars.

JUNE 18

New Mexico, 2015, age 55

Loneliness tugged me into her bedroom
Sheets lavender as the night we had that fire
She's a bitch, but you never know until she's left you ensconced in her smoke
I held my breath long enough to keep her out, yet she came
Soft music pretending to soothe me, lulling me into her furnace
Karen says, 'Such a sad affair,' but I know her touch, her skin against mine, nuzzling me awake
My dreams save me each day long enough to douse my embers with wine

Walking now, awake and breathless
Lest she take residence here inside me and burn

JUNE 19

Colorado, 2024, age 64

I believe in past lives. My dreams inform me much the same way the waking life informs others. I've had dreams of rescuing loved ones from captivity; I've taken bullets and fought in many wars. All my life, I've measured my strength by how much I could endure, and endure I did. The ways I squared off with my father, the chaos I endured with my schizophrenic mother, the sacrifice of my family during the cult years—just to name a few. Having warrior blood in my veins is something I feel with conviction. My life has been a mission, a battle, a test of strength at every turn. Each time I faced death and overcame my foe, it fed the warrior in me. The scars I've worn as a badge of courage.

Now I know that the victory is in walking away. I don't judge myself for the life I've led … I just want a different life now. I'm tired of fighting. I'm not sure what made me a soldier, but I'm finished. I'm laying down my blade and buckler to learn a new way.

JUNE 20

New Mexico 2014, age 54

These words flow through me …

"Close your eyes now, child. Your needs are coming to you. Your needs, your desires, your wants … all are here now. Give your heart to the wind and the sun, the rain and the thirst. Give your love to yourself, for there is no other. And if you cry, I am here to catch your water. We'll store your tears in a tiny earthen vase. And if you laugh, it will feed me. And if you scorn me, I will not falter. We are the same. Behind you, it comes … all that is to come. Do not be afraid."

Summer

Reflections on Summer

SACRED SOUTH

Young warrior, strong and agile, you are the Summer of my youth. Your heart is that of the wolf, and no task is too great for your strength and bravery. As the noonday sun reaches its peak of brilliance, so are you at yours. You are the eagle's flight that knows no contest. Summer Warrior, this is your season for action and precision. You are the fire, the energy, and the creative force that keeps all living beings alive and vital. Passion is the crest upon your chest, for this is your moment to thrive.

JUNE 21

Indiana, 1971, age 11

Dad built a bedroom in the basement, and now my brothers live down there. It's pretty amazing to have a room down there, and sometimes Jesse lets me lie on his bed and listen to music on his headphones. The music through his headset is so much better than anything I've ever heard. I love Jesse so much, and the best part of being down there is being with him. It really is the best place to be in the house.

Today was really special because he showed me the ring that he's going to give to his girlfriend. He's going to ask her to marry him, and I'm the first one he told. I think that's pretty cool, but I'm sad to think he will be leaving home. I don't know how I am going to survive without him. He's the best friend I have.

JUNE 22

Colorado, 2010, age 50

Center place of Earth, Heaven, and In-between, you abide with me as I abide on the good red road. I walk rooted in you. The birds rest upon my branches. When the strong north winds of my mother blow, I set my leaves to sail, as we are all a dancing family. My gift to you is myself, ever abiding in this cycle of life. Reaching toward your heaven while grounded in your grace.

JUNE 23

California, 2004, age 44

I started having pains in my chest, so I ran to the ER. I thought I was having a heart attack, but they found nothing wrong with my body. The on-call doctor suggested I start going to therapy.

A friend of mine highly recommended Dr. Bob in Dana Point, so I called him up, and now I see him once a week. Dr. Bob is of medium build with a little extra around the middle. He has a shock of white hair, and one of his eyes strays a bit. Dr. Bob is a seriously tough guy. According to our mutual friend, he used to be the therapist for an East LA gang. I don't suppose anything I say will surprise him.

I've been talking a lot about Jerry because he seems to be the source of my anxiety. Dr. Bob hates Jerry. He says if he is ever diagnosed with a fatal disease, he has a short list of people he will *off* before he dies, and Jerry is now on that list. I believe him, but I hope it never comes to that.

The last time I went to see him, he decided we were going to do a playacting exercise. He said it would really help me. Dr. Bob sat on a chair in the middle of his office, and then he put his hands behind his back like they were tied. This is how it went:

"Jubilee, I want you to pretend I am Jerry."

"What? No. I'm not sure I can do this."

"You can do it. Imagine you are in a half-dome metal building (it's called a Quonset Hut), and Jerry is sitting just like this, on a chair, and tied to a pole behind his back." He kept his hands behind his back while he was talking to me.

"Okay, I'll try," I said.

"You really need to do this. There is nothing else in this shed ... just you and Jerry, and he can't hurt you anymore. Do you understand?"

I sighed heavily.

"In your hand is a machine gun, and you are going to kill Jerry. I am Jerry now, and you need to do this."

At that point, I was sure I could not pretend to shoot Jerry, but then Dr. Bob started insulting me and calling me names .... It was horrible. He didn't really sound like Jerry; he just sounded like a guy trying to sound like Jerry, but I needed this to stop, so I pulled the trigger of my imaginary machine gun and filled him with pretend holes. Dr. Bob flailed to his death. I was not impressed, and I knew Jerry was still alive. I felt sick.

I don't think this helped me. This is not my idea of healing. **Jubilee tip: Therapy should be therapeutic.**

117

JUNE 24

New Mexico, 2016, age 56

Today was a day of working outside. My son-in-law has built a rather elaborate chicken coop that is still evolving, and as one might imagine, making a chicken yard that is coyote-hawk-and-owl proof in southern New Mexico is a real accomplishment. My granddaughter, Luna, is three and equally obsessed with her chickens and the movie *Moana*—so much so that she named two of them Maui and Moana. Today, we played with them, cleaned their water, and gave them fresh feed.

As my daughter and granddaughter were taking care of the feathered little darlings, I saw a rattlesnake sliding by only a few feet from where I was standing. I quietly asked my daughter to get Luna and move away quickly.

She grabbed Luna, and we all headed to the house. Simone put on my viper boots, and Lorraine grabbed the sidearm. She and Simone headed back outside together. I stayed with Luna as we watched from the porch.

"Is Grandma gonna gun the snake?"

"I hope not, honey; we don't like to gun animals."

"Is the snake gonna kill Maui?

"I sure hope not, sweetheart."

"I hope Grandma guns the snake."

"Honey, let's not think about that."

"Gun it, Grandma, gun it!"

Three shots fired. I took a long sigh.

(shit).

"I guess Grandma had to gun the snake."

JUNE 25

Kansas, 2020, age 60

COVID-19 is still with us. We have had several family members meet the virus and combat it. At one point, we thought we might lose our sister-in-law. She was intubated for twenty-seven days before they decided to place a tube through an opening in her neck to help with breathing and remove liquid from her lungs. They also treated her with plasma therapy antibodies. Every treatment was experimental, and no one knew if she would make it. She was one of the first people to survive being intubated and isolated for so long. Finally, we got her back.

She returned home on May 20, 2020, and her release was covered by the Indianapolis News on Channel 13. The following Saturday, Lorraine and I organized a parade to celebrate her survival. There was a firetruck, police escorts, and many decorated cars; we honked, threw gifts into the yard, and screamed with delight!

We are all still very apprehensive about being in public places. Not much is known about this disease. Its way of choosing victims is mysterious and selective. God's face is in it, as with all things in nature. Each day I pray for safety and guidance to navigate this new world. I hold no judgment for those who choose this time to leave. Even though we must all go at some point, I would like to stay.

JUNE 26

New Mexico, 2013, age 53

Each morning I rise, anticipating your aroma
My ritual groove brings me nearer to your grounds
Walking quickly, turning the corner, you are there
Your smile, my gentle sigh, your eyes meet mine
I know you have what I'm looking for
Each day you know just what I need, and you know my brew
Somehow you anticipate my challenges
My burn rate
My need to get through one more day
Never too much, and always just enough
Your expertise entices me to return to you each morning

You dare to care about who you are to me and let me witness
your alchemy
Your steam, froth, and foam delight me
There, I said it
I love you, my barista.

JUNE 27

Indiana, 1967, age 7

My best friend and I were playing out in her yard today when my
brother Doug came screaming down her driveway on his bike. He
hit the rock that's shaped like a turtle and went flying into the air. I
saw the bike wheel fly off and go into the bushes, and Doug just lay
there bleeding. My friend and I ran over to see if he was okay, and it
looked like his front teeth were all pushed to the back of his mouth.
I followed him into the house, and as he looked into the mirror, I
could see him pull his teeth back into place. Yuck! He is so lucky
he didn't break his neck and die, but that's my brother. He's kinda
crazy that way.
Jubilee tip: Put things back where they belong.

JUNE 28

Indiana, 1976, age 17

These railroad tracks wanna take me. God, I want to get out of
here so bad. *Just walk.* I can balance on the rails, no problem. Shit, I
can even jump from one to the other without falling. I can almost
run on them.

When I see the train coming, I wait until the last minute before
I let it go on by. When I hear the whistle blow at the Sunnyside
crossing, I know the train will be here soon. I want to feel the
vibration of the wheels' rumble, so I place my ear on the track. I
think I can feel it, but I'm still waiting and not afraid. This train
and me, we've been together a long time. I guess if I keep walking,
I'll end up in downtown Indianapolis someplace. *Find a boxcar and
live in that.* I'll be out in the country if I go in the other direction.

Either way, I have no place to go, but I need to go. Staying here is killing me.

Jubilee tip: Moving doesn't always fix it.

JUNE 29

Michigan, 2009, age 49

Our youngest sister, Mindy, convinced all ten siblings and my dad that having a week-long vacation at Lake Pickerel in Newaygo, Michigan, would be the most fantastic thing we have ever done as a family. Right. Mindy could sell a hat to the Pope. Damn, she's good. So, this is day one at The Great Given Family Vacation, oh my.

This morning it didn't take long to figure out that Kastle Inn Resort was an electrical fire waiting to happen. No shit, someone got shocked by a faulty electrical socket, which blew the circuit. Brother Jesse came to the rescue and mended it with a stick of gum and a paperclip. Ha, just kidding, but he is that kind of guy. Jesse can fix most anything. In reality, this place is old and maybe a death trap. No amount of paint and daisy decals are going to fix it.

I feel fortunate to be in the Bird House. I'm pretty sure it's the best dorm in the camp. The toilets work and aren't backing up into the shower like they are down the hill. (Take a moment here to understand just how bad that is.) There's a sense of being above the danger up here. Down the hill, along with the bad dorm, are three tents of various sizes holding a dozen or so of my nieces and nephews and their young children. This is an epic Given family gathering.

I'm sharing a rather small room that has a single bed and an old bunk bed. Barb is on the top bunk, brother Jesse and his wife took the full mattress on the bottom, and I am on the single pushed up against the wall. It's somewhat reminiscent of our childhood, which we all swore we would never ever do again, yet here we are. I suppose it's different when you do a thing on purpose—most things are like that.

For the record, brothers Daniel and Mark along with their very tidy wives spent one night down the hill and unanimously agreed to seek other lodging. It was not surprising when they announced they were going into town to stay at a charming little bed and breakfast. We tough kids decided this would be too good to miss and stayed in solidarity. I will also say for the record because I am sure most of my siblings are thinking it:

Damn, Mindy, you should get an award for this!

JUNE 30

Michigan, 2009, age 49

Day two at Lake Pickerel. The best part about this place is spending time outside. There's a shuffleboard, so Jesse and I played, and that was pretty cool. It was a little more difficult to "shuffle" in the rain, but it was still fun. We each won a game, and then we went on to make a campfire—while the rain continued. It was big fun standing around the fire with umbrellas—my kind of fun. Jesse had a trash can lid over his head, always unique.

Now I am in my little bed, PC in my lap, the last to go to sleep. I should be more tired than I am, but I had coffee, so it may be a while before I nod off. It's a symphony of breathing in here. I'm glad we are all related.

Somebody just farted … jeez, I hope it doesn't stink. Well, now we have a full-on snore-fest in this little cracker-box room … wow, how lovely. I'm going to go pee and try to drift off. This should be an exciting week indeed.

JULY 1

California, 1980, age 20

Granger has duty today aboard the USS Pollack. His boatmates picked me up so I'm not alone and said they had a job for me to do. I was kinda excited to be part of a project they were working on. We three went across the peninsula from the Mare Island Naval Base, where the USS Pollack is docked alongside the USS Nautilus, which is being decommissioned. My job was to write the letters "FTN" on this giant balloon that Jackson and Tim would inflate.

Since the USS Nautilus is being decommissioned, all the stuff on board is getting tossed in the garbage. The guys decided to grab some of the fun stuff and bring it home. One of the things they got was an emergency antennae kit. It works by activating a canister by putting it into the water. The canister then blows up this giant balloon that floats into the air with a wire attached. This becomes an emergency antenna.

So, here I am, writing these giant letters on the side of this huge balloon across the bay of the Naval Base. Then, as the balloon is floating up, up, up into the air, the guys tell me that these letters stand for "Fuck the Navy." Meanwhile, across the bay, Granger is watching the whole thing through the periscope from the USS Pollack submarine while his commanding officer is standing right behind him.

"What's so interesting, Granger?"

"Nothing, sir, nothing at all."

They all love me more now, and I'm hoping I don't get arrested.

Jubilee tip: Ask questions before writing giant letters on a military balloon.

JULY 2

Colorado, 2011, age 51

Today, as I was looking through some old work of mine, I found a poem that I wrote when I was twenty years old. I had also incorporated the verse into a watercolor painting. The painting was of my fist with gnarly vines growing through my fingers. Back then, I remember feeling such discomfort in my chest that I started calling it my *black hole*. I was experiencing deep anxiety and depression, but there was no help for me, so I wrote to try and alleviate the pain. This is the poem I wrote:

In the fist of a stranger lies the heart of my soul.

He grasps it like a vise, and I can hardly breathe through the fingers of his confinement.

The vines of my effort start leaking through his grip.

If I grow, will he let go?

Should I win his favor so he will open his hand to the light?

Should I fight his tightening hold so I can live to know the right?

How can I fight this strain of bondage with my seed planted in his fist of fury?

I will grow—I will grow to no measure, and he will fall away with the shell of my seed.

I will grow so that he may not know the hold on my soul.

Even my roots will be too immense for his grip, and he will be swept away by the wind.

I'll be free then, but for now, if I grow, will he let go?

As I look back and remember those desperate feelings, I'm so incredibly grateful the *black hole* has subsided. Therapy and having children have helped, but I still struggle with anxiety and depression, just not as often. It makes a big difference to have a professional to talk to. Even more so, I have not given up, and I never will.

JULY 3

Michigan, 2009, age 49

Day five at Lake Pickerel. It's Friday morning, and the nieces made fresh doughnuts, plain and sugared. One of the girls brought them up to the Bird House. They are delicious.

So far this week, I have spent time with my family—lots of time with my family. Yesterday, my brother Sam and I took the kayaks and explored a new lake where there was an island called Turtle Island. The history is that the Native Americans gathered clay from that place to fashion their pots. There was a no-trespassing sign, so we just docked and ate our crackers and cheese. Then we rowed furiously back to the campsite just for the fun of it.

Last night I threw the football with the guys and Mindy. It felt great to do that.

Sister Barb took off fishing to see if she could catch anything with her soon-to-be-expired fishing license—I think there are only thirty-seven minutes left. The campfire still burns—we've kept it going for the past four days. Someone always tends the fire until the wee hours of the morning. Then, some of us are up with the sun, so it hasn't been all that difficult to keep it burning all the time.

My dad's up and seems to be doing okay. It's hard to tell with him. He's a fragile guy these days. He'll be eighty-nine in a few weeks. Honestly, I don't think his frailty is so much about his age as it is about his state of mind since Mom died this past January. Memories of Mom tend to send him south fast. I think there's a delicate balance there with him. We all talk about Mom, and so does he, but it doesn't take him long to get lost in the abyss of his memories. I wonder what those thoughts look like because I know he was a real jerk to her. The last thing I want to do is get inside my dad's mind. From where I stand, it looks and feels pretty dark. I almost feel bad for him, but I don't.

Brother Jesse is still in bed; how I love him. My niece seems to be using a surfboard as a kayak. Looks like fun—I might try that. My other niece is taking pictures. My brother-in-law went downstairs to talk shit since no one upstairs was listening to him. The young mothers are itching to go home, as the week has just about run out. Uh oh, now a baby is crying. Everyone is tired of having fun.

JULY 4

Michigan, 2009, age 49

Due to the faulty electrical wiring, the coffee pot in the Bird House takes about an hour to make coffee. After Jesse rewired the electrical circuit, we gained a few minutes of speed. I'm pretty sure waiting that long for coffee has been the worst part of this week for me … and of course, everyone else is waiting for it too. I could stay here for another three days if the coffee pot would just perform.

Sister Mindy took her son to the doctor because she thinks he has strep throat, and I am still in my pajamas writing while looking out the window from my perch of the Bird House.

Lorraine is coming today, and that is a really good thing. Most of the family thinks she is a friend who bought Mom's keyboard—which she is. Lorraine is also my new girlfriend, and I love her. I hope my family loves her too.

~

My Lorraine flew into Grand Rapids, and I went to get her. It was so good to see her. We enjoyed a beautiful drive back to the camp. She met the family members who were still there. I wondered then what they thought. It seemed a little strange at times having someone new there. They were all just getting accustomed to me being with Dee, and then along comes a "friend" and, of course, no Dee. Everyone pretty much knows now that Dee and I are split. It has been a slow process for me to let everyone know that I am dating Lorraine now. I'll admit, I'm a little afraid they'll think I ran to the next available person. I get the feeling they think I'm scared to be on my own. After spending fourteen years in a religious cult, I wonder what they think about me. It has been very strange for me to participate in family gatherings and make decisions for myself. I wonder, too, what being on my own might look like. Regardless, everything is still so new to me, and I'm doing the best I can. Maybe it doesn't matter what anybody thinks; maybe it only matters what I think. I know I love Lorraine and that I want to be with her. Welcome to the Given Family.

JULY 5

California, 2005, age 45

This self-doubt I'm struggling with makes me feel so insecure. Then, I get afraid and start people pleasing, and I've made some incredibly bad decisions in that space. Now I feel trapped again. Over and over I do this. Fear, doubt, fawn, and freeze. And then trapped. What is wrong with me? I hate this, and I wish so much that I could sit in my own skin and be okay.

JULY 6

California, 2004, age 44

On the 405 from Aliso Viejo to Irvine, I head to work. As I drive and in my sleepy head, I write this poem:

I rode to work on fumes today
My tired eyes out of gas
I slept with my eyes open while following the car in front of me
Which just so happened to be going in the same direction
The coffee pot was on my mind
But I just couldn't seem to get out of bed with you
Last night I knew you needed me to take you in my arms
As your eyes met mine, the darkness hid nothing
Pressing up against you never felt so warm
If I had it to do over again, nothing would change
You could not have been more beautiful than you were

JULY 7

Colorado, 2010, age 50

My friend Linda is mad as fuck at me. Seeing as how I've been having an affair with her partner, Lorraine, and now we're openly dating, I can get how she might be just a little peeved. Secrets can be really toxic sometimes. What I've come to learn is that I didn't fool anyone. Just because I tried to hide my relationship with Lorraine didn't mean it was hidden. I think the worst part was trying to pass off an affair as a friendship while everyone involved suspected differently. I was constantly calling my friends liars when it was me who was lying.

It's safe to say that Linda no longer wants to have anything to do with me.

Jubilee tip: Just because you have your reasons doesn't mean they're good reasons.

JULY 8

Colorado, 2019, age 59

I would really like to have someone to spiritually connect with. I get so weary of wanting this. I have my wife, Lorraine, and she's wonderful; it isn't that I'm alone. I just feel such a longing inside myself to find a like soul. Someone who sees me from the inside out. A soul friend. I've sought it with my medicine women teachers, and yet I haven't become part of that day-to-day community. I've looked at my blood family, but we're just too different. Maybe there's no one like this for me. Maybe it's just an unreasonable desire. My medicine woman says I may need to get used to being a lone wolf. I guess this is what earth life can be like. I must say I feel so lonely sometimes.

JULY 9

Indiana, 1978, age 18

Day by day, I seem to grow weaker. Something is eating away at my inner being. The harder I fight, the deeper I cut, the more this savage beast feasts on my existence. I should have dominion over this beast, but I don't. It's stronger than me, yet a part of me. I hate it with such an intense passion that if I could separate it from myself, I would surely torture it to its death. Oh, to have the knowledge to overpower this creature of pain. An army of a million soldiers couldn't capture or kill this enemy of my heart, soul, and mind. Still within me lay the oceans of tears I have never cried. Should I release them, they may drown me, they may kill me ... but maybe they may set me free.

Jubilee tip: Ask for help when you need it.

JULY 10

Indiana, 1969, age 9

The sounds of the ice cream truck's tinkling music sent me racing through the screen door. I ran to my mother begging.

"Can I *please* have a quarter for the ice cream truck, *pleeeease?* I have to hurry before he leaves."

Today is my lucky day … ice cream is happening, and now I feel like anything in the world is possible.

Thanks, Mom … thanks, God. Thanks, ice cream truck!

JULY 11

New Mexico, 2016, age 56

My petition to the South in my medicine circle:

"If you would be so kind, please give me strength in this body. Show me the physical strength of a warrior in this vessel. Grant me health and vitality and make me the warrior I am."

"It feels good to be your friend," I hear the voice of the South flow through me …

"Root here, find yourself on this land, and see where you have come from. You need not fear me anymore, Jubilee. I know you saw your mother wounded by the South, and I know you saw your daughter killed in the South, but I am not here to harm you. There is a path for you now; the way is soft, warm, sunny, and shaded. It goes up and down, and you will be satisfied. I am your friend. Come into my rest and peace and see my fire, vitality, and strength as your own."

JULY 12 (12)

Indiana, 1976, age 16

I listened to Barbara Jordan's speech tonight on the TV. I'm glad my dad wasn't home tonight. There is no way he would have let me watch this. My dad really doesn't like colored people. She was speaking at the Democratic National Convention, and Walter Cronkite was reporting on it. She quoted Abraham Lincoln at the end, and I can't get it off my mind.

"'As I would not be a slave, so I would not be a master.'" She said, quoting Lincoln from his personal notes. Maybe this is what democracy means … no slaves and no masters … just people working together for the good of everyone. Seeing a strong black woman giving this amazing speech was so cool. She is powerful. I think if God were a woman, She would sound just like Barbara Jordan. **Jubilee tip: Live like God is a strong black woman.**

JULY 13

New Mexico, 2017, age 57

Today, we packed the trailer for our move to Colorado. I'll be so glad when we pull out of here and get these kids to a more civilized place. We had a close call as a haboob came rolling toward us from the Caballo Mountains. A haboob is more than a dust storm. It is a giant fucking wall of desert sand moved by high winds. This one was going to be seriously bad.

As the storm hit us, I watched my daughter manage the heroic feat of single-handedly lifting an easy chair onto the trailer. Then I noticed my granddaughter running loose and screamed, "Grab the baby!"

My son-in-law grabbed Luna and ran for cover. The wind hit us with such force that all we could do was hold on, keep our mouths shut, and pray nothing hit us. This is life in the desert, and it can hurt here. It is time to move on.

JULY 14

Rhode Island and Providence Plantations, 1985, age 25

Today was a terribly hot day, so I took the girls over to our neighbor's house to get cooled off. They have a small child's pool that's perfect for Molly and Hannah. Even so, I have to keep a strict eye on Molly … she wants to do everything her sister does even if she doesn't know how.

The water in the kiddy pool wasn't deep, and I was in the pool with them … but I got distracted by a short conversation with my friend for only a few seconds, and then I turned back to see Molly silently floating in the water beside me.

There was no cry for help and no sound whatsoever. Instantly,

I reached for her and pulled her to the surface. My heart was pounding as I witnessed what could have easily been the end of her sweet life. Molly spitted and sputtered and gasped for air, and I sat in shock as the shadow of her end passed over me. I thanked God that in that instant her life was spared and I got a crash course on how to be a better mother.

As I think about it now, I am haunted. How can something so devastatingly permanent as death be so silent?

Jubilee tip: Never look away from a child in water.

JULY 15

New Mexico, 2017, age 57

Today, we tried to roll out of New Mexico. I have mixed feelings about leaving. My sense of urgency to get out of town has been for my daughter and her family … they've been miserable here. But I'm leaving so much that I have built behind me. The restaurant, the murals, the community, and some of my best friends. It's a lot to walk away from. There are legends about this land that say this place will spit you out if you don't belong here, but it can be hard to leave if the land wants you to stay.

Lorraine and I were pulling a flatbed trailer, loaded with an old Ford truck. The old truck has a large metal cage built on its bed, and that's where our dogs, Trouble and Nan, were settled for the long haul to Colorado. Our Great Dane, Jasper, sat with Lorraine and me in the cab of the truck we were driving. My daughter and granddaughter were following us.

We were just barely out of town when one of the tires on the trailer blew out.

"Shit!" Lorraine shouted.

"What happened?"

"The goddamn tire blew!" She was pissed.

We pulled off onto the side of the Interstate. Lorraine jumped out of our truck to assess the damage. She said we would have to take the flat off, unhook the trailer, and drive back into town for a new tire. Nan and Trouble were barking non-stop at each passing vehicle from the back of the old Ford. My daughter and grand-daughter were parked behind us and waiting for instructions.

No problem. Soon we headed back into town to get the new tire. Once in the automotive department at Walmart, we found out we had to buy four tires because the specific tire we needed was only being sold as a set.

"For fucks sake." Lorraine was not happy.

We bought three new jacks and returned to the scene by the side of the Interstate to remove all four wheels from the trailer. Then we went back a second time to Walmart so they could put the new tires on all four wheels. The dogs were losing their minds at this point. Simone and Luna were getting hungry.

We were halfway through the tire debacle on I-25 with barking dogs and 80 MPH cars screaming by, and that's when the weather hit. The wind picked up hard and fast, to the point of shaking the entire operation. Then the rain … the pouring rain. Lorraine hates being cold and wet. It wasn't really cold, but it was definitely wet, dirty, windy and nasty. She was not having fun. As I watched her in her dirty jeans and soiled shirt, she kinda reminded me of a soaked little badger. God love her for doing most of the work. I don't recall ever seeing her that mad before.

As I looked back at the mountain and the land through all the noise, wind, and rain, I had a realization. Something was holding us there. It was as if a hand from that mountain reached out and touched my shoulder. It felt personal. Lorraine was still changing tires. I took a deep breath, bent over, grabbed a fistful of dirt, and prayed.

"Spirit of the land, I've been a good steward to you, and you have been kind to me. I ask you today to please let me go. I need to take my daughter's family from here. I'll come back to visit, but please, please, I need to go."

As we finally pulled out of there, I felt the kind of calm that said I didn't need to look back.

Jubilee tip: Always respect the land.

JULY 16 (13)

Connecticut, 1999, age 39

John F. Kennedy, Jr., died today. The plane he was flying crashed into the Atlantic Ocean on the way to Martha's Vineyard. He and his wife and his wife's sister all died. I really liked him. He seemed like he wanted a different life from the political life of his family. He took a stab at acting and made his acting debut on Molly's birthday, August 4. I remember the day his father was shot and killed. I was four years old then. It was on his third birthday when one of the saddest photographs in history was taken: John-John saluting his father's casket. It's so strange the way things happen. He was so young and handsome, with the world entirely available to him, and now he's gone.

When people talk about God, why *God* lets things happen and how *God* didn't stop this or that, it makes me wonder how much we're making up this God character. No one really knows what is being said by God—I dare say, no one knows a thing about it. We are all just speculating. What if we're all obtaining what we want by intention? What if we're using prayer and willpower to manipulate outcomes? Right now, I am compelled to pray to something greater than myself as though it were a homing beacon within me, but truly, I sometimes wonder if I'm the creator of my own life, and what if John-John was too?

Then I think, oh shit, that's heresy. I play with this scenario in my mind so much, but then I feel guilty for doubting the one true God. I need proof that the saints and prophets knew the truth about God. I need to know the God of the Bible exists. I need this truth so badly that I would do pretty much anything to have it.

Jubilee tip: More than one thing can be true at the same time.

JULY 17

Colorado, 2017, age 57

My dad's birthday is today. He's ninety-seven years old. I some-times wonder how it is that he has lived this long. I suppose there is a lot to say about genetics. I've also heard that assholes live forever. My dad has been a real asshole most of the time. This isn't to say that Dad doesn't seem to have redeeming qualities … he will do things that could be considered nice. One of my favorite things he used to do was take Mom for a ride when she needed to get out of the house. I love that memory.

"Dad?" Mom would say, "Let's go for a ride."

Then he would lace up his shoes and get her to the car. My dad knew pretty much every road and all the history of our hometown, and I believe those drives soothed Mom's nerves. He could be nice like that sometimes.

Happy birthday, Dad. I sure hope this is the year you stop being a jerk. Mom's gone now, but I hope you'll keep trying anyway.

Jubilee tip: It's never too late to stop being an ass.

JULY 18

Indiana, 1968, age 8

Have you ever had one of those crazy moments where you think something is happening in the world that will change your life in the future, but in that moment, that's all you know? It almost feels like that thing people call déjà vu. Or when the science teacher says that I could be looking at a star on any given night and it could have already burned out over one hundred years ago. He says that's because it takes the light longer than one hundred years to travel to where I'm standing. Or even when I hold a seed in my hand and know that there could be a tree hiding inside of it. These feelings, I swear they're happening to me just now.

Summer

JULY 19

Colorado, 2011, age 51

Today, I wrote this about someone I would later marry.

When we first met, you were aloof

There was something about the way your cowboy boots matched your hair

You always looked the other way when you drank your beer, playing hard to know

You were waiting on your girlfriend, and it was about to snow

You said she was the funny one

Little did I know then you would be my lover

There was something about your boots and your hair

Though, come to find out, it was more about your heart

The one who came to know mine, so hard to know

JULY 20

New Mexico, 2013, age 53

I am lying here next to you

You are reading your new book, not minding my nudges

It is dark now, and my arm is over your waist

The elixir of your breath gives me space to float

Your lips press against mine, launching me onto a quiet lake, drifting

Doors open, and you are gone now, though remaining my sentinel

Such comfort blankets me and keeps me while sleep imitates death

Sleep well, Lorraine

JULY 21

Colorado, 2024, age 64

Today, as I was listening to a book titled *The Exvangelicals* by Sarah McCammon, she spoke about her white evangelical upbringing. As she spoke, I related to a few of her experiences. One of those she mentioned was her childhood fear of the rapture. I chuckled to myself about how real that was. The rapture was such a big deal to me as a kid. I still get angry over having been held over hell like a hotdog, so to speak. How do reasonably minded people still believe these Biblical stories are true?

I remember my dad driving us around, looking into the sky, pointing at a jet stream saying, "Look up there ... you see that A?" We looked up, and sure enough, there was a giant white A in the sky. My dad went on, "That's a sign. Do you know what that stands for?"

We had no idea.

"Anytime," he said. "Jesus is coming back anytime."

I had a sick feeling in the pit of my stomach. I was kind of excited but mostly afraid. The rapture was the great unknown that had me constantly on watch.

I remember coming home from the sixth grade one time to an empty house. I would have been twelve years old. It was unusual for the house to be empty, so naturally, I thought the rapture had happened and I was left behind. My heart nearly lept out of my body. I looked everywhere frantically, and no one was there. I was alone and sure I was doomed. Terrified. Now what do I do? Then someone came home, and then shock turned into relief. Jesus hadn't actually come, but the fear was still there. It was hard to think I was good enough for Jesus when I didn't feel good at all.

JULY 22

Connecticut, 1996, age 36

My daughter and I are going roller skating tonight, and I can hardly wait. We *love* skating together.

Jerry must take me through the drill before we go.

"I want you to be mindful of those wanting to make sexual advances towards you."

"Okay, I will. I always do."

"No, you don't. You are careless, and you don't think. You must be aware of your surroundings and feel the energies directed toward you."

"Right, I'll do my best. I really do try to pay attention."

"Here, I want you to wear this while you're there—it will help shield you."

"A wedding ring?"

"Wear it on your wedding finger, and it will protect you. It won't work unless you pay attention. I'm counting on you. You must understand that you place others' lives in danger if you don't do exactly what I am telling you. Anyone who comes after you comes after me, and this is something *Dad* and my *brother* will not tolerate. You know this."

"Right, I remember. Okay, I promise I won't let you down."

Jerry speaks about God and Jesus being his dad and brother. I think he wants to remind me what the punishment will be if I fail.

I remember when two guys came to our church, and one of them asked me out on a date. I tried to be nice to him—I thanked him and told him I wasn't interested, but Jerry said I encouraged the young man, and a week later, that man committed suicide. Jerry said Dad was upset by my actions and these sorts of things will happen when lines are crossed. He said I needed to be more careful unless I wanted to take responsibility for losing more lives.

I am so afraid of someone else being hurt. That guy was really nice to me. I think the ring is a good idea.

Jubilee tip: Jealousy and protection are different things.

JULY 23

New Mexico, 2013, age 53

A poem for Molly.

I turned my head while ten of your years had passed in the afterlife

It isn't the same here as it is for you—still

I long for you to hear me

Close your eyes for a year
As I sigh and watch
Your breathing thoughts
Dissipate into the web
Just past your vision
I'm sitting here watching you
Would that your heart could touch mine once more
Our essence could fly entwined
We could laugh from the belly of our love and hunger no more
Believe me when I say I am there with you, my daughter
Such a thin veil between us
But time is playing his game, his sleight of hand
Don't you believe it; it isn't real
What is real is what you feel
I miss you, my Molly

JULY 24

Indiana, 1968, age 9

It's a warm day today, and Mom and I are sitting out on the porch. She has a hat and a sweater on.

I said to her, "Mom, aren't you warm wearing a sweater?"

"Oh no, I have to stay covered."

"Why?"

"I'm allergic to the sun," she said. My mom has the most beautiful brown skin, and I can't understand for the life of me how she can be allergic to the sun.

I look at my own skin and wonder what would happen if I got allergic too.

I asked her, "What will happen if the sun hits you?"

She just looked at me and said, "Never you mind, I just can't."

JULY 25

Kansas, 2020, age 60

I had the most amazing experience. As I was in a private group on social media reading the posts, I noticed a unique name. It rang in me like a familiar call. Abra. After looking at the conversations around this person, I reached out, and we began corresponding. Today, I asked her to be my soul companion, and she said yes. I've never done anything quite like this before. It feels like the door to my heart has been swung wide open, and finally … finally, there might be someone out there who can share my soul's journey. **Jubilee tip: Don't give up on life, Lone Wolf.**

JULY 26

New Mexico, 2015, age 55

As I prayed today, I heard the flowing voice of the Great Spirit come to me.

"You feel pain as though it were an unwelcome stranger. Your compassion for humanity's physical pain has taken a strong leap. You shouldn't give up your quest for well-being even though it feels so far away. The lesson is well-being, no matter what the physical condition. Will you do it? Will you be willing to let happiness settle upon your unrest? Will you continue to let joy and peace be your companions through your searing pain? You have it in you … it is as natural as breathing. Remember this and you will go far, Jubilee."

JULY 27

Colorado, 2024, age 64

For four years, I have been living alongside my soul companion, Abra. During that time, she finished her doctoral thesis and completed her PhD. We've moved several times and are soon to move again. Our bond as soul companions has deepened, strengthened, and survived tests and challenges. We are still exploring what this relationship can be and do. Soul companions … we're both new at this.

For me, Abra has a wisdom that is like no other I have ever encountered. There are times when she speaks privately to me that I swear she is channelling a beloved saint from long ago. Her love for me is unselfish, caring, and transparent. Her eyes reflect a kind of intelligence she can scarcely contain. We are alike in the ways that are most important to me and as different as the years that separate us. It baffles me, but somehow our age difference doesn't hinder the connection I share with her.

When we are alone, Abra sees me in a way no one else does. She touches my soul in such a way that it brings out all the parts of me that otherwise would not have expression … the playful child, the young man, the nurturing mother, the lover. Oh, she knows my faults and has seen me lie, stumble, and fail, but she continues to believe in me and to trust me.

When I see her out in the world, she lights up almost every person she meets, unless they are a sour curmudgeon and unable to be moved. Her goodness is reflected in the food she cooks and the animals she cares for. She's an artist in the way she moves, and that moves me. She also loves a good debate and doesn't shy away from a heated conversation. Her activist spark is genuine. She is kind and generous, and I love her.

JULY 28

Colorado, 2022, age 62

Today, I felt as though a heavy weight was trying to root me into the cushions of my couch. Moving through space took as much effort as swimming in cold honey, yet I did it. The last time I felt like that, something was dreadfully wrong. Maybe I'm having an off day and nothing is wrong at all. I went to Denver to see my body worker, and she seemed worried about me.

"Jubilee, I've never seen you like this. Are you okay?"

"I don't know. I'm just really having a low day."

Little did I know that one of my dearest friends and former business partner, Tory, was lying on a hospital bed in Las Cruces, New

Mexico, preparing to pass from this world to the next. I'll receive this news tomorrow morning, and yet, in that moment, my body knew something traumatic was happening. *Am I connected to her soul?*

What is intuition, really? Is it the radio receivers of our cosmic alien cells constantly feeding us information about the unseen world? Is it God speaking in a quiet voice? Are they the same thing? I stand in awe of the seen and unseen world we live in as I navigate this phenomenon.

Jubilee tip: There is no separation between us and those we love.

JULY 29
Colorado, 2009, age 49

You are looking out of my eyes, and I am looking back at you through me in you.

JULY 30
Colorado, 2007, age 47

Showing up in a romantic relationship after spending a decade and a half in a cult has been hard. I don't even know what I am doing half the time. I really am doing the best I can, but I just don't know how normal people act. My wife has an explosive temper, and although it isn't nearly as bad as what I was used to with Jerry, I just don't want to do it anymore. I've built a fortress of protection around me, but I know this isn't right.

Just because I don't fight back doesn't mean you can continue to abuse me. I'm not perfect, but I'm trying so hard. Stop yelling at me and taking your aggression out on me. Stop it!

Dee can't seem to help herself. What am I, her whipping post? Each time I don't fight back, she thinks I'm saying that she's right ... whatever it is she's raging about.

I can't take this again. Don't point your tongue at me like a weapon anymore ... I'm done.

Jubilee tip: Silence is not consent.

The Tell

JULY 31

Indiana, 1972, age 12

I remember a few years ago spying on my older brother Mark as he came home from work. He sat on the living room couch with his head in his hands. Peeking from around the corner, I watched him take our big German Bible and look through it as though he were searching for something. Soon he shut the book and put it back in its place, laid back, and stared at the ceiling. He sighed heavily. I knew he hadn't found what he was looking for.

A few months later I heard a loud noise outside, and I ran out through the front door. *What was that?* Someone was running up the road screaming "There's been a crash … it's Mark!" I'll never forget it for as long as I live. I looked down the street to see my brother caught between the metal folds of his mangled car. He had hit a tree.

It took two wreckers pulling the car apart for them to finally get him out. He was really messed up. His leg was busted to bits, and his arm was broken, and his lungs were punctured, and they said his spleen was ripped clear in half. Later, they said he died for a whole minute before they brought him back. I wonder if he met God.

He was in the hospital for months, and then he finally came home. While he was recovering, I could hear him scream at the top of his lungs because he was in so much pain. He even punched a hole in his bedroom wall out of frustration. He was suffering. Later, I heard him saying this crash was what it took for him to turn his head to God. The hand of God, he said it was. I think those days of looking into the Bible and searching were somehow answered in this crash. I wonder if finding God has to be like this. I sure hope not.

Summer

AUGUST 1

Colorado, 2017, age 57

Today is Tuesday, and the air is warm in the shade. I hear the ravens caw, caw, caw. They perch before me, and I am kin to them. As mated pairs, they keep each other company in their curiosity. There is a green bucket with water in the yard, and they often stop there. I love them. This place is a healing haven, and I am in awe of the magic of the music from the wind in the pines, the humming-birds' flight, and the sound of my own heart beating. I'm pretty sure the Great Spirit is here.

AUGUST 2

Illinois, 1979, age 19

It's been a long night, and my dream … it was so vivid it's hard to believe it was a dream. It was just so real—so haunting. Can a dream be so real that it becomes something else? Maybe a sign or a vision? That's how I feel about this dream.

There was a deadly storm at sea. I was in it on a boat. As I clung to the side rails, all I knew was that if I made it to the cabin door, I would be safe. I crawled toward that door against pouring rain, wind, and waves crashing over me. I grabbed and held onto anything that would keep me from being cast into the ocean. When I finally reached the door, I clutched at it with both hands, feeling relief for an instant. Then the wind under my feet grabbed the door, ripped it from its hinges, and cast us both into the furious sea.

I woke up sweating as my heart was pounding wildly in my chest. *Dear God, I'm safe,* I kept thinking.

Nearly afraid to go back to sleep, I put my head back on my moist pillow.

Then the dream began again. It was the very same. Lightning pierced through the wind's crashing sheets of rain. Claps of thunder rumbled through me, commanding me to survive. Once again, I believed the cabin door would save me, and I was compelled to grope for anything secure. I reached the safety of the door only to be thrown again into the sea. I clung to the door, but it was useless. I was doomed to be swallowed by the maelstrom. This happened three times before I was able to rest. It was torture. What could this possibly mean?

AUGUST 3

Connecticut, 1994, age 34

Jerry sat on the porch smoking a cigar while drinking his scotch ... a double on the rocks, and he began ... "I am the angel who wrestled with Jacob. I am Gaia. I am Death. Da'at from the sefirot I am. I created you, and to me, you will return."

Jerry handed me a dog tag etched with stars representing Earth, Arcturus, and the three sisters constellation. There was a line connecting Earth to Arcturus, and Jerry said it was a map guiding me back to where I was born and back to him.

"Take this so you will know how to return to me should we ever be separated."

"Okay," I said.

He sat in silence and then asked me to leave because *they* were coming, and he didn't want me to be hurt. He told me *they* were celestial beings who were not fond of humans and were highly protective of him.

I walked away in awe, clutching my dog tag star map.

AUGUST 4

Rhode Island and Providence Plantations, 1983, age 23

My second baby was born today. Granger and I named her Molly Jean after his mother. It's also the name of a character who played in a movie we both loved. I hardly had any labor pains with Molly, and she arrived before I made it to the delivery room. Granger almost missed it. She is twenty-two inches long and has the most beautiful olive skin. Her hair looks to be blonde, and she is beautiful.

Molly isn't anything at all like Hannah was when she was born.

She has an entirely different look and feel about her. I am feeling something intense and strange, and I can't quite lay my finger on it. It's not that I don't love her because I do. I hold her, and I feel something foreign and severe. I'm almost afraid of her. I just don't know what to make of it.

AUGUST 5

New Mexico, 2013, age 53

Remembering my darling Molly today:

We took a walk through the old graveyard. You were four years old, do you remember? You said you knew why the little stones were there. "They're baby baseball players!" you said because the initials on those tiny memorials looked like what you had seen on baseball uniforms. Beautiful and innocent you were that day.

I think about all the times you came running with awkward bumps and bruises. I remember your smiles, your almond eyes holding your precious soul. I remember laying with you until you fell asleep because your stomach wouldn't let you rest. So much of you still resides within me.

My love for you burns as a beacon in my chest. Come now and reach through this ephemeral curtain and take my hand. Let us try again—let us be that which should have been. My sweet Molly. The day you were born and the feeling that came washing through me ... I had no idea it was telling me I would have you for such a short time. I miss you so much, my little angel.

AUGUST 6

New Mexico, 2012, age 52

This morning I awoke next to Lorraine while she was still sleeping. I looked at her and saw a mirror version of her face floating above her. While the sleeping Lorraine's eyes were closed, the mirror version's eyes were open, gazing at her ... their noses almost touching. As I watched curiously, the mirrored image slowly faded.

I wonder if I will ever understand these visions. I may never know what they mean and why they come to me. Still, I muse over why others don't see what I see and why I see them at all.

AUGUST 7

Indiana, 1968, age 8

I've never been to a real movie theater before because Mom and Dad say it's bad to go there. I sure wish I could go and see the movies the other kids get to see. I'm in third grade, and my teacher is Mrs. Durfee. She's pretty nice, and today she played a film for the class. I love it when we get to watch films, and I really love how it all works. The light shines through the film, and then we watch the picture move on the screen. It amazes me. So, today was Jiminy Cricket singing about safety.

"I'm no fool, no-siree, I'ma gonna live to be a hundred and three. I'll play safe for you and meee, 'cause I'm no fool!"

I think he was singing about being a winner because Jiminy seems like a winner to me, and I want to be safe so I can be like that. I sure do love Jiminy Cricket and want to live to be one hundred and three!

AUGUST 8

Connecticut, 1996, age 36

Today, as we were inching our way through the Bess Eaton Coffee drive-through, Jerry said to me, "You have more trust in your brakes than you do in God."

I quickly realized he didn't want me to keep my foot on the brake while I was waiting on the two cars ahead of us and it had something to do with my faith in God. So, I placed the car in park at each and every momentary pause. By doing so, I tried to show Jerry that I was a good student.

Sometimes Jerry's lessons make no sense to me. I get frustrated because I don't have Jerry's higher mind. I'm trying to understand these lessons, but I feel so inadequate.

Jubilee tip: It's good to have faith in your brakes.

Summer

AUGUST 9 (14)

Indiana, 1974, age 14

President Nixon quit today—he did something called Watergate, but he says he's not a criminal. I don't know what Nixon did, but it feels like he made a big mistake, and when you're the President of the United States, mistakes don't just go away. He's still giving the peace sign, so maybe it's not that bad.

AUGUST 10

Kansas, 2020, age 60

Darkness can become a companion if given a chance. Insidious and cunning, this lesser expression of being disguises itself as something justified. The longer it's allowed to walk beside you, the more at home it becomes, and then as if by accident, it will take residence within you. Thoughts are like wheels in constant motion whirling through the cosmos, so be aware. Don't be ignorant about this ... it is no accident—it's a deadly courtship. Negativity will take you over if you allow it to.

AUGUST 11

New Mexico, 2013, age 53

Today, my granddaughter Luna was born. I remember when Luna's mom was born and how excited I was. It was such a natural thing to try and see the world as a better place through the life of my daughter. I wonder if Simone is seeing the same thing through her own newborn's eyes. There is such hope in new life that unless you have had a child pass through you and held them in your arms, you might never experience it like this. It's much like having a warm light glow in your heart and knowing that as long as this magical phenomenon of birth happens, there's a chance this world will continue to get better.

AUGUST 12

California, 2025, age 65

Prayers are my bones, blood, and breath. The raven's confirmation, the warning of the hawk, the hummingbird's insistence of who I am.

The infant smile, my sister's hug, and my lover's breasts. All prayers that save me.

AUGUST 13 (15)

Indiana, 1968, age 8

I'm worried my brothers will have to go and fight in the Vietnam War. Some of their church friends have gone, and I can see they are wondering if they will have to go too. Mom and Dad are talking to them about making sure they get into college. I guess, if the boys are in school, they might not get drafted. I hope they don't have to go. I don't want them to die.

AUGUST 14

New Mexico, 2014, age 54

Today, I am driving to Ohio to spend the weekend with my sisters. Every year we take turns at each other's houses. We call it the Annual Given Sisters' Reunion. This year it's my sister Barb's turn to host the five of us, and we're going to have such a great time. I love my sisters so much. I can hardly wait to be with them.

AUGUST 15

Ohio, 2014, age 54

I received word today that the man who held me captive for so many years is dead. It was a brutal suicide death where he stabbed himself in the heart and sliced his own throat before falling from the balcony two and a half stories up. The effect of this news moved through me in such a way that it felt as though my essence was coming loose from my body. How many times did he say he created and owned me, and now it feels like he's trying to take me with him. *I believe I might be dying.*

AUGUST 16

Ohio, 2014, age 54

Something is wrong with me because I don't know who I am exactly. I'm not sure how I got here. My sisters say the car in the drive is mine, but it isn't—I don't even like it. How did I even get here? My sisters say I own a restaurant, but that doesn't seem real. I know my sisters, and I know the car outside is hideous—why would I buy a car that color? I see my dead mother, and there's also someone else standing there. Is it an angel? Am I dying? They tell me Lorraine is coming, and I remember her, but I have no sense of time. Some force is trying to take me out of my body, and I feel like I should be afraid, but I'm not.

AUGUST 17

Ohio, 2014, age 54

Lorraine is here. She got here so fast! As soon as she walked through the door, she put one hand on my forehead and the other on the back of my neck. Looking directly into my eyes, she asked me some questions. I saw her, but I didn't know all the answers. I knew her, though, and it felt good to be with her. I wonder how she got here so fast. All my sisters look like familiar strangers. My youngest sister, Mindy, showed me a timeline she drew of my journey here, yet it's nothing I recognized. It looked like a drawing with strange shapes and pictures ... none of it made any sense to me.

Then, my sister Jennifer was on the phone with Blossom, my medicine woman, while I sat on the grass in the backyard. Blossom instructed my sisters to build a prayer circle. While they placed the stones around me, starting in the East, a single yellow maple leaf fell beside me—I knew it was Molly. I remember Molly.

Jennifer handed me the phone, and Blossom asked,

"Jubilee, do you know who I am?"

"Yes."

"Do you want to live?"

"Yes, I do."

She repeated, "Do you want to live?"

"I do. I want to live."

"Say it again."

"I want to live."

Jubilee tip: Don't die today.

AUGUST 18

New Mexico, 2015, age 55

So many times I've experienced premonitions. My dreams, my thoughts, and visions ... all of these seem to speak to me as if reality were not as linear as we believe it to be. I daydream about these things.

I'm confident there is no such thing as empty space. How is it when I think of you, you call me? How do I know what you will say just before you say it? Can we hear each other's thoughts? We can't prove all this connectivity yet, but that doesn't matter to me. I know it's true. The distance between you and me is filled with an intelligence that rides on the invisible impulses of our focus and intention. Do you doubt this? Go on, think of me, and see if I call.

AUGUST 19

Indiana, 1963, age 3

My mommy won't touch me, so I am holding onto the hem of her dress and crying.

"Mommy, I don't like you like this."

My mom won't look down at me. She just stares out the window with her hand on her face.

I just don't understand what's wrong with my mommy.

AUGUST 20

Colorado, 2024, age 64

It's late summer, and this book is nearly finished. These memories feel like clothes put on the line to dry. Each garment has its own story, and every once in a while, they all need to be washed and aired. Some are worn out and will go to the rag bin. Those I won't mention again after recording them here.

By now, you know I was a tomboy who struggled with becoming a girl, and then I was a captive young woman who only wanted to please God. Eventually, my innate desire for women allowed a door to open so that I could walk into a new life. I've been the one who has had the courage and strength to face down a schizophrenic mother, a violent father, a cult leader, and a less-than-ideal God. I have suffered great loss and have nearly died, but my angels have been kind to me. My faith is now secure. I believe in the benevolence of Creation. There is order in my world, and I feel loved and cared for. I've finally decided to stop hiding and simply tell the truth.

And as the ravens cry and the hawks soar and the little birds defend and dive, so am I on this planet at ease.

AUGUST 21 (16)

Indiana, 1972, age 12

My brother told me today that Jane Fonda was a communist. I know she's an actress, but I didn't know she was a communist. That seems like a really bad thing. But I saw a picture of her with some guns and Vietnamese people, and they were all smiling like they were friends, so maybe it's true.

AUGUST 22

Connecticut, 1999, age 39

Jerry said it was time to spar, so we got the padded swords out of the umbrella stand by the front door. I hate these lessons, but he says I have to learn self-defense. He hardly ever hurts me, but he always scares the shit out of me.

He came at me hard and fast, and although it wasn't nearly as frightening as having his fist thrown at my face, it took every skill I had to avoid being hit by his padded bat. Suddenly he dropped to the floor and looked up at me like he had been hurt. I was perplexed. Then he hooked his foot around the back of my ankle and pushed on the front of my knee with his other foot. I went down hard to avoid breaking my leg.

That fucking hurt, you bastard! I didn't dare say out loud.

"See? That is how you take down your assailant if you are on the ground and vulnerable."

"Thanks, that really works," I murmured.

I hate him sometimes.

Jubilee tip: Don't let a jerk show you self-defense.

AUGUST 23 (17)

California, 1981, age 21

Granger and I are staying in Vacaville for a while with our good friend Tim because the fires are blazing near our apartment in Vallejo. The smoke is so thick and heavy it's hard to breathe, and the sun looks like a hot red ball in the sky. The smoke doesn't bother me so much as knowing Charles Manson is in prison right here in this same town. I remember when all those horrible cult murders happened, and knowing he's so close gives me a tight feeling in my chest. I feel afraid just thinking about it. There really are men like that in the world, and no one can see them coming until it is too late. I don't know why that makes me so scared, but it does.

AUGUST 24

New Mexico, 2014, age 54

Jerry has been dead for just over a week now. One of the members of the cult reached out to me to let me know he had connected with Jerry's brother. From all that his brother shared, I am now convinced Jerry's life was nothing but lies.

Everything was a lie. All the stories Jerry told over and over again were lies. How the military watched him. How he had been one of Admiral Rickover's whiz kids. That Strom Thurmond was best friends with his grandfather. His pet bobcats and so many more stories that I heard repeatedly for years. He made it all up.

I'm in shock.

He made us keep the televisions on twenty-four hours a day for years because the house was bugged and under surveillance. His twin siblings died in a car crash, but he walked away from the same incident miraculously unharmed. His double doctorates from Oxford, the military secrets, the fucking sound gun he tortured me with …. He was a god and knew the secrets to this life and the life to come. All lies. I'm sick with grief. I'm sick with regrets. I'm sick with sadness over the life I gave to him. Why didn't I see it sooner? Why?

Jubilee tip: There are some things in life you will never understand.

AUGUST 25

Kansas, 2020, age 60

I can do nothing about what has already transpired in my life. Some of it has been out of my control, and some not. I've made a few insane choices that have wreaked extreme havoc in the lives of my loved ones.

Many times I have acted out of fear. Other times I acted selfishly. There were times I was brave and times I was a coward. Regardless of how it all went down, I did all I could in those moments to make the best choice for myself and my family.

I continue to count heavily on the grace of the Great Spirit I have come to know. I try and keep humility and gratitude as my constant companions—and between you and me, I see myself as a piss-poor student of life. To those I have injured, I'm so sorry.

AUGUST 26

Connecticut, 1991, age 31

Dear God, where would you have me go today? What would you have me do? I lay down my burden to you and ask if you would grant me the ability to walk the path you have set before me with courage and strength. I know the gentle tug of your guidance within my heart, and although I may walk alone, I will go.

AUGUST 27

Rhode Island and Providence Plantation, 1987, age 28

My life isn't like other people's. I see things that others don't. It doesn't happen all the time, and sometimes it is just a flash but this experience was altogether different. This time the vision inter-acted with the physical world.

This morning early, while Granger and I were still sleeping on our waterbed, I awoke to see a long-haired dog jump through our closed bedroom window into the room. We live in a beach house, and our bedroom is on the second story. The dog had a long snout—it looked alien. The dog stared directly at me as it walked over to my husband's bedside. This strange dog bit him in the leg. Granger jumped in his sleep while grabbing his leg and yelled, "Ouch!" Then, the dog looked at me again before jumping back out the closed window. I sat up in bed and wondered what it was I just witnessed.

So, later this morning, I asked my husband what had happened to him in the night. He tried to reason there could have been a mosquito or a shard of metal, so I told him what I saw. He didn't hesitate to say I was crazy and that there was no way in hell that could have been real, so I decided I wouldn't share this kind of thing with him again. Ever. I do wonder how it is that I saw what I saw—I know it was real, and no one can convince me otherwise.

Summer

AUGUST 28 (18)

Indiana, 1963, age 3

Walter Cronkite is talking on the news tonight. Something is going on that my dad says "just isn't right." Mr. Cronkite is talking about black people being in Washington, DC, and there's a colored preacher preaching, and he is talking about having a dream about all people being equal, and that's just like the song I sing in Sunday School about Jesus loving all the little children ... *all the little children of the world.* I love that song. *Red and yellow, black and white ... they're all precious in his sight.*

The preacher sounds so nice to me, and I think everything he says is good. My dad just sits in his chair and says, "There's nothing good about this," but I don't understand why he's so mad. When Dad gets angry, his hands turn into fists. He sure is scary when he's like this.

Mom is sitting in her chair, rocking really fast, and then she stops.

"Dad, can we turn this off?"

He gets up and turns off the television.

AUGUST 29

California, 1980, age 20

When Granger has duty days, Jackson usually comes over. We smoke pot, then we play the black and red game. He pulls out the deck of cards and holds them up one at a time, and I tell him whether it is black or red. I love that he gets so tickled and laughs so hard because I'm pretty good at it. He thinks I'm psychic. We have a lot of fun together, and I like his company. It really is nice to have someone here with me on these long, lonely days.

Jubilee tip: Friends are good.

AUGUST 30

California, 2004, age 44

My girlfriend, Dee, wrote this poem for me. I love her.
Amber waves of silken
Lava flowing gold veils
Around my face
The barest touch against
Lips full, with promises
Of delight, tender mischief
She leaps from above
To take me in the night
Teeth and talons and passion's fruit
Tame the ache of flesh and quench my thirst
In the candle's flame, I now always see
The tigress eyes in the trees

AUGUST 31

California, 2004, age 44

I found the woman of my dreams waiting for me in the Single Gays section of the San Diego Online Personals. Her name is Dee. Our first meeting was electric as we talked about our families and how we got to where we were in life. We were smiling with our eyes the entire time. She had beautiful hair, a sensuous mouth, and smelled like something so heavenly that all I wanted to do was get closer to her. Then there was the first side-by-side walk. I entertained the brief notion of brushing up against her arm (by accident, of course). Her lacy black bra teased me through her slightly unbuttoned starched white shirt. All of this became the makings of a pretty good day at the beach.

After our first date, I went to see the Kahuna woman in Hawaii for a month. Dee and I talked and wrote to each other and continued to get to know one another from afar ... and then the month was over. I was so excited to get back to San Diego so I could see her again.

I wasn't thinking about sex, but I was definitely thinking about thinking about it. Being a grown woman and not a feverish school-girl, I wanted things to be done properly and at the right time, but honestly, I was afraid because I had never been allowed to be with a woman *all the way* like this. I've had sex with women before, it isn't that. It's just that all of my encounters were done in secret, and I've had to hide this aspect of myself. I love women, and until now, the thought of having a life as a lesbian has been out of my reach.

Dee knows nothing about the cult yet, and the apprehension around telling her is staggering for me. I know I will tell her, but I don't want to scare her away. I just want to live a normal life and, yes, to have sex.

SEPTEMBER 1

California, 2004, age 44

When our hands first met, the energy danced between our fingers, and I felt a tender sexual arousal. Then our eye contact drew us closer.

And we kissed.

Our first kiss sweetly introduced the texture of her lips to mine. It was like kissing rose petals, and the loveliness of that moment was not to be compared. Her breath mingled with mine, and I felt lifted into a space of longing.

SEPTEMBER 2

Colorado, 2010, age 50

I miss the parts of her that I love.

SEPTEMBER 3

New Mexico, 2016, age 56

The transformation of my soul has not been my own doing. I believe some celestial trickster has coaxed and prodded me through this life. Is it possible I've not had a choice all along?

Jubilee tip: Choice is all you have.

SEPTEMBER 4

New Mexico, 2017, age 57

It's been five years of owning and operating Prickly Pear Café in this sleepy desert town. The work Tory and I have done, along with Lorraine's contribution, has turned this place into a hub for our community. We've hosted private dinner parties, we've sold dozens of artists' tabletops, we've had disco dances and open mic events, and don't forget the stoned spelling bee on New Year's Eve.

The community loves us, and I have a sense of completion knowing I did a good thing for this town and for my friend. Tory has fulfilled her dream of sharing ownership in the restaurant business. I have had great coffee and a lot of fun, too, but now it is time to hand it over to Tory and go on to something else. It's been my privilege to show my art, pour drinks, and create a lovely space for our town. I know Tory is going to continue to do great things.

Happy sailing, Prickly Passionistas, I love you all very much!

SEPTEMBER 5

North Carolina, 2020, age 60

A rock that has a sediment line all the way through it is a wishing rock. If you find one, hold it securely in your hands and make your wish. It will come true. I have mine in the palm of my hand now, and I am wishing with all my heart.

SEPTEMBER 6

North Carolina, 2020, age 60

Never underestimate the power of your soul to inform your destiny. Ponder this.

SEPTEMBER 7

Colorado, 2009, age 49

I am a traveler, neither born nor dead in any fashion or way. If the fears of death are rooted in me, I might as well say I am a pawn upon this planet and throw my experience to the wind of fate.

Fear of this kind can go so far as to create its own world of ideas, vernacular, and superstitions passed down through generations and bloodlines until we need another Christ to come.

I believe in life and life everlasting.

I asked Lorraine, "How do you suppose God was born?"

"He wasn't," she said.

This, to me, was the perfect answer.

SEPTEMBER 8

California, 2004, age 44

Dee and I have been together for six months now. My experience of sex and intimacy has been so much different than any relationship I've had with a man. Emotions are much more intense.

Being tender with a woman has laid my heart wide open, but when the pangs of apprehension, guilt, and self-consciousness enter my mind, they rob me of joy and sexual pleasure.

I'm discovering sex beyond the heterosexual experience. There is a level of intimacy that transcends gender, and now I go there with my lover. I'll never feel guilty again.

She is beautiful in my eyes, and all I want is to experience her.

SEPTEMBER 9

California, 2004, age 44

For my wife ...

Lips that the sweetest touch should ever taste are yours

Shoulders silken smooth invite the day that should never end

Of breath and wet upon velvet skin

Eyes that gaze on beauty so rare

This is you

SEPTEMBER 10

New Mexico, 2022, age 62

"Let your weaknesses surprise you. It's better than anticipating them."

Abra

The Tell

2001, Connecticut, age 41

All day today, the TVs in every room replayed the scene of jet planes crashing into the Twin Towers in New York City. My brother Mark and his wife are there, and no one has heard from them. I live just an hour's drive away in Connecticut, so it's close enough to feel the living threat of what's happening. All I can do is keep my eyes on the televisions and try to figure out this devastating attack. *Why did this happen? How did this happen? What's coming next?* I feel the pain and sorrow for the increasing number of victims, and my brother and his wife are somewhere in that cloud of ash. I'm calling everyone I know who may have heard from them. All we can do now is wait and pray.

~

This evening, I finally heard that my brother and his wife are safe. My sister-in-law is in the Sloan Kettering Cancer Hospital recovering from surgery, but my brother Mark is literally running everywhere because there's no public transit. Ash has covered the city, and people are afraid—so many are dead. Mark has been staying at the hospitality house across the street from Station #1, and it's reported that every firefighter from that station is dead. Mark said he just talked to so many of them last night, and now they have all died. I think he's in shock. We all are. The entire country is reeling from the impact of this assault. My first instinct today was to get my daughter out of school and keep her close to me. I don't know what will come next, but it feels as though a war has begun.

SEPTEMBER 12

Indiana, 1974, age 14

Since I turned 14, I have thought a lot about the church stories I've been told all these years. In order for the Jesus story to work like they say, then I have to have started out a sinner. If I wasn't born bad, then there would be no reason for him to die up on the cross the way he did. I wish it weren't like that because I was already born into a bad situation with my dad being pretty mean and my mom being really sick. Pile all that on top of my being born a sinner, and I really don't know what chance I have in this world. I know they say all I have to do is ask for forgiveness, and then he'll swoop in, clean things up in me, and then lead me on to have a good sin-free life. None of this can I actually see. What I don't understand is why I need someone who lived a thousand or so years ago to help me make a decision to be good. Everyone wants the same thing, Jesus or no Jesus. Don't get me wrong, I'm sure Jesus was amazing. I actually really like what I know about him. Maybe there's something about it I'm missing. I'm just a kid trying to figure things out.

Jubilee tip: Jesus didn't believe in original sin. He was Jewish.

SEPTEMBER 13

Connecticut, 1995, age 35

The only way I can journal is to write in code because I can't risk Jerry finding my writings. Every word I write, each thought I have is subject to scrutiny. The following is a passage from one of my journal entries about a church member I've known for a little while. I would love to get to know him better. I feel like he and I could be something really special.

"My heart has looked upon another with a smile. Finding another seeking soul is so rare. Intimacy is like a dark cloud looming over my head, and all I touch becomes rained upon or dead. It has always been this way. I wonder if it will always be.

"My boundaries are set, and I dare not venture into realms of affection or friendship. Still, the art of obedience has me somewhat baffled. The voice of God? Let me just say there have been false alarms. My soul is so resourceful and cunning that I often fool myself into a spiral of imaginative divine guidance. Or is it? Oh, to know the actual voice of God so surely there could be no doubt. Jerry is my guide, and how I long to learn as he has shown me.

Being disobedient and displeasing is something I can barely think about. My straying eyes may damn me. Pain upon pain echoes within me at the whisper of his displeasure. My heart looks to God for strength.

"Dear God, wash me clean of my desires. I only want to be pleasing to You."

SEPTEMBER 14

Colorado, 2016, age 56

Today, Arlene and Kitty are getting legally married. I'm presiding over the ceremony, and it's my honor to wed together our best friends or our "other wives," as we call each other. Our Great Dane, Jasper, is wearing his red bow tie and walking in with Lorraine to stand as best gal and dog. The brides are beautiful and handsome. We are all in black tuxedos, and it's all so very gay! To have friends who are family is so important, and this bond is one I will always cherish.

SEPTEMBER 15 (20)

Indiana, 1963, age 3

I'm so little, and I never know much about what's happening around me.

I heard my mom say, "Dad, why do you suppose they put that bomb in a church where children could get hurt?"

The radio was talking about an explosion in Birmingham, Alabama.

"Mom, you and I both know there isn't going to be any peace."

Mom didn't say anything.

Dad continued, "If I ever catch any of our kids carrying on with a black person, I'll disown them. So, how do you think these bombings are happening?"

My dad really doesn't like black people, and it scares me when he gets like this.

Jubilee tip: Children learn from what they see.

SEPTEMBER 16

California, 1980, age 20

Today, Granger and I, along with his two buddies from the submarine, drove their station wagon to Reno, Nevada, from our place in Vallejo. The wagon had hardly any brakes, so Granger had to pump the brake pedal hard to get it to stop, and none of the dash instruments worked either, so Granger had to shake the car to tell how much gas was in it. He also had to guess how fast we were going and for sure try and avoid big hills.

So, there we were, at the Chapel of the Bells with our two submarine buddies. The minister worked a circuit of chapels going from one to the next to marry as many couples as possible, so when he showed up, he was late and out of breath.

I wore slacks and a shirt. Granger wore gray pants, a white shirt, and a gray sweater. He looked nice, so I took a picture of him at the gas station, but none were taken of me. The day is over now, and we're back in our apartment. The apartments here are named Roosevelt's Terrace, but everyone just calls them *Garbage Gardens* because they're nothing fancy at all. It was an exciting day, for sure, and Granger's buddies were fun. I think they were excited to be with us and have a day off from the boat. I'm tired now and will turn in for the night. I guess I'm married now.

SEPTEMBER 17

Connecticut, 2003, age 43

Jerry really has a lot of nerve. Yesterday, he showed me a printout of a document signed by the founder of the Universal Life Church, Kirby James Hensley. The letter stated that Dr. Jerry Teach was being ordained as the new leader and acting Pope of this worldwide, far-reaching organization. As I stood there looking at this document, Jerry began explaining to me that he was changing his title to John Cardinal Teach. My first reaction was astonishment and disbelief. How could this giant leap have happened so suddenly? I looked at the paper and read it again. Sure enough, it was signed by Kirby, and it said all the things.

"Congratulations," I said hesitantly. There was an unsettled feeling rising up in me.

Jerry looked at me with a direct and intense gaze, half smiled, and said, "This is going to change everything."

This morning, I dialed up the modem and went online to see what I could find out about Kirby and his organization. The search engine brought up a few pages, and as I was scrolling through them, I saw his death notice. I gasped.

Kirby died on March 19, 1999, so unless he is risen from the dead or some other Kirby is now the leader of this organization, Jerry is lying.

Shit.

I've seen Jerry steal money. I've seen him try to cheat the mob, and I've seen him fake heart attacks. But this, this is something completely insane.

That document was fabricated, falsified; Kirby's signature, forged. If I confront him, there's no telling what he will do. I was already scared of him, but now I am not even sure what he is capable of.

Jubilee tip: Don't believe a liar ... ever.

SEPTEMBER 18

Connecticut, 2001, age 41

Our world is still shaking over the destruction of the Twin Towers. My brother and sister-in-law are still in New York City, waiting to leave, still in shock at what has happened. Today, I am considering what must have gone through the mind of a random person working in one of the Twin Towers—the same day that ended so many lives. This is what I've journaled:

Today, the sun is bright, and hope is given to those whose ambition is early to rise ... but this is the day to sleep in. Feeling the pull against gravity as the elevator goes higher and higher ... feeling a sense of climbing the ladder of success. A coworker's blue tie brings thoughts of passing holidays and what would be the right gift for Dad this Christmas. As the doors open to a new day, the mind becomes focused, and the work begins—on this last day.

Coffee is never so right as it is at the start of a new day, and today it seemed sweeter somehow. Just after the thought of the first refill, an incredible sound whips through each body with such force that no one can decide to fight or fly. "What was that?" Fear turns to panic, and then every memory that might store the answer for escape flashes through every mind. Still waiting. Looking at each other to see if someone had found the answer. Still waiting. Another thundering bash is heard, but this time it is also seen. The companion building is hit, and now there are screams and smoke and fire. Frantically grasping for the cell phone and dialing quickly and accurately, the call is answered. Only a few words say it right, and there are only a few seconds to say it, still—it doesn't seem like enough. "I love you. I love you."

SEPTEMBER 19

New Mexico, 2020, age 60

My dear friend Sulo is dying of cancer. She's sitting in a worn-out recliner with swollen legs elevated, looking at me. We had talked some months ago about her thoughts regarding self-election, and at that time, I didn't truly understand she was this near to transitioning. Her DNR envelope is taped to the wall beside her. Her eyes are leaning into an altered reality. Her feet seem planted in two worlds, and now I know she will be passing soon. Abra is here with me. As we sit here with my dying friend, I feel as if she is peering through a thin veil, and her words have an eerie significance.

My marriage with Lorraine is in trouble. I recently met Abra, and we're exploring our connection as soul companions.

I asked Sulo if she could see anything concerning my relationship with Lorraine. She said, "I think there's going to be some big changes. They're going to be more than location, and I'm not sure ... I'm not sure ..."

She became emotional and started to cry. I reached to hold her arm ...

"You don't have to say," I tried to comfort her. "... but is it something I need to know?"

"I think it might look different, but it won't be different with you and Lorraine ... the love will still be there and might look different in a blossoming unbelievable way ... it's more that I see changes in Lorraine that she doesn't realize are coming. They're going to be good."

"That's good," I said.

"... you're going to go through this too, Jubilee, and you're going to realize in little ways and in long, long ways ..."

I was searching for insights.

She rocked in her chair, nodded her head, and began to laugh. Her eyes knowingly looked at me as we leaned into an embrace.

In her ear, I whispered, "I love you so much."

"I love you too ... and Lorraine."

"I know you do."

As we left, I knew that would be the last time I would see her.

SEPTEMBER 20

New Mexico, 2023, age 63

Last time I was in Indiana, my brother-in-law confronted me. He asked if I was worried knowing I was an abomination to God and was going to burn in hell for being a lesbian. He said it so matter-of-factly, as though he was certain of my condition. My first reaction was anger, but then I cried. I'm not sure if I cried because of the insult to my humanity or because I felt so alienated from my family. He's an asshole and will say anything, but what I know is that most of my family feels the same way. They just won't say anything because they love me. This patriarchal domination god from a book written by men centuries ago is not my life or my belief system.

I felt like I was standing in the kitchen one more time listening to my mother telling me I was going to hell tonight because God was whispering it in her ear.

Bring your God to me for a chat, dear brother-in-law, or anyone else who thinks they can tell me the mind of God. I'll even buy Him lunch. If your God can show up and tell me I'm a Sapphic heathen, then I might listen to Him. You have my number … I'll make time.

Jubilee tip: "This above all: to thine own self be true …"

(Act 1 Scene 3 of Shakespeare's play, *Hamlet.*)

SEPTEMBER 21 (21)

Indiana, 1975, age 15

They finally rescued or caught Patty Hearst. I'm not sure which it is because, first, she was kidnapped and, then, she was robbing banks. They say she was brainwashed. *I wonder how that happens.* I mean, I can see how she could think she might escape if she went along with what her kidnappers wanted her to do, but how did they convince her that being a criminal would be a good idea after locking her up and hurting her? I wonder what she was thinking. Brainwashing is such a strange idea to me.

Jubilee tip: Sometimes strange things happen.

Autumn

Reflections on Autumn

SACRED WEST

Hello, my old friend. We have come through so much together, haven't we? You have been with me through thick and thin, and I love you as my own soul. Why is it that in the West, I hold on to my past like it was my lifeblood? The Thunderbird is flying overhead to wash me clean.

Jubilee, leave your hardships for the Earth ... her rocks and roots will tend to your mulch. There is a harvest to be reaped and stored. What shall I leave my children? I won't find grain or vegetables in my wounds, and as I have heard you whisper in my ear so many times before ... *Your problems will never point you to where you want to be, daughter. Watered by forgiveness, the fruit of your labor is in the deep and abiding love you have come to gather. Stay there until your final hours, and your children will be left with an inheritance that will never fade.*

So quickly the seasons change, and now it is time for the bears to yawn and the fallen leaves to be food and a blanket for my mother. My journey has been a good one, and I have loved and been loved, and so it was worth it all.

SEPTEMBER 22

Colorado, 2019, age 59

My youngest granddaughter was born today. Her dad calls her "Thumper." He says she jumped right out of my daughter and into his arms when she was born. Once again, we have a baby born on the cusp of a seasonal change. My Hannah, then her sweet Wednesday, and now our precious little "Thumper." Oh, how I love these little darlings … all of them. I do wonder about the timing of these young ones. Come to think about it, I would have come full term on the summer solstice with Simone, but I was afraid of being too far from the hospital and induced her to come earlier. Forgive me, Simone; I just couldn't wait that long to hold you. I believe all of my children and grandchildren were right on time.

SEPTEMBER 23

Colorado, 2009, age 49

Autumn bends to reflection
What fun we had in early summer
The undertow didn't have a chance to win me over
Plenty of times, I drifted out to sea
Yours was an island I found whose beach, sandy white, and palms delighted me
Brown and wet, we basked
Alas, the waters of Makapu'u nearly had me, and we drifted apart in its beautiful rage
Life, you are my vessel
I am your breath
Slippery as you seem, no destination disappoints
No sea succumbs to winter's reflection
As well, nor do I

SEPTEMBER 24

New Mexico, 2022, age 62

God just started talking to me today ...

"Jubilee, do you know the difference between dark and light?"

"I think I do, yes."

"Tell me, please."

"In the light, I can see clearly."

"And in the dark?"

"The dark forces me to use other senses in order to navigate, and it frightens me."

"What frightens you about it?"

"I can't see what is there, and I'm afraid something might hurt me."

"So, you're afraid of something that might be there?"

"Yes, I guess you could say that."

"What if you could see something harmful in the light—would that also frighten you?"

"Yes, but at least then I might be able to do something about it."

"If you don't mind my asking, what senses do you use to get around in the dark?"

"I use my sense of touch and my sense of knowing."

"Would you say the dark helps these senses become stronger?"

"Yes, I definitely would say so.

"This has been a most helpful talk."

"Anytime, God."

Jubilee tip: God is cool.

SEPTEMBER 25

Connecticut, 1994, age 34

Walking down to the shore and over the hill, I see the boats, the docks, and the homes nestled into the hillside. This is the path I take every day, and just where the road winds down to the level of the water, there, down the embankment is that rock where I sit to cry. My struggle is with God and Jerry. How do I show up as a cheerful servant when my whole life has walked away from me? I have no spiritual agency to empower me. All I know is a blind and obedient compliance.

Jerry speaks of St. John of the Cross and his dark night of the soul, and he compares my lot with him so I can gain strength and insight, but there's nothing in this story to help me. My sorrow has consumed my breath … I miss my children so much, and yet I must serve God because if nothing else, I am God's beloved.

SEPTEMBER 26

Colorado, 2010, age 50

I've been living a lie for over a year. Having an affair behind Dee's back has weighed so heavily on me that lately, I question whether or not I deserve to live. Having a secret like that has been unbearable. Then I had to build lies around our secret, and the lies became their own reality. Am I no better than Jerry and every other liar I've known? I'm so incredibly stuck.

I've struggled with suicidal thoughts before but not since I was a teen. Today, I am wondering if the world would be better for everyone if I just left. The gun in my hand isn't loaded, but when I hold it to my head, I know it could be. I wonder if Molly thought these same thoughts before she pulled the trigger. It must have been different since her gun was loaded. I sense her presence with me, and the feelings of her regret swirl through me in such a way that tells me this isn't the way to go. I hurt so bad, and I can't see my way out. God, please help me.

SEPTEMBER 27

Indiana, 1976, age 16

There are many places to hide in the dark unless the one I am hiding from isn't using her eyes to find me.

"Go to bed, Mother, and leave me alone; the devil has already come for me."

Autumn

This endless schizophrenic haunt sends me to hell every night.

SEPTEMBER 28

New Mexico, 2021, age 61

Sometimes the only way to win a game is to change the game. The game changed for me when I met her. She is exquisite, and although I am sixty-one years old, parts and pieces of me are coming alive like a passionate young woman. At times I feel like a young, playful girl, then a warrior and a little old man at other times ... but always, the woman in charge of this house knows I am struck by love.

She moves like the grace and power of the ocean ... all while making tea. My head tilts into her neck, and I breathe her essence, and it fills me with so much desire I blush. She leans into me, and all I want is to take her into me. When I am chilled to the bone, her words pour over me like the sun's healing rays. When we make love, she moves my body in waves of ecstasy. She knows my language, and I know hers, and yet we are divinely unique. She gives me room to breathe and to grow, but there is no gap between us. If I had to put one phrase to her and me, it would be that she knows how to receive me and I, her. One might think it unlikely to have this experience at my age, but I can't be bothered with that. It has happened. The game has changed, and I have won.

SEPTEMBER 29

New Mexico, 2012, age 52

When I was a child, Mom said there were gates in heaven like rich people have, only they were made of pearls. She said that the streets were made of gold and that she didn't think animals go to heaven, and I thought that was a shame, especially since she loved cats and birds so much.

I asked my mother, "If you could have anything in this world, anything at all, what would it be?" She said she would have a screened-in porch off the back of the house. The simplicity of this grand wish made me love my mom more than I can say—her heart was so good. Looking back, I don't think her life had a lot of pearls or gold. She's gone now, but I wonder, if Mom could choose again, if she would trade the giant pearly gates and golden freeways to live her final days at home with Dad, her kids, maybe a stray cat or two, looking through catalogs with pictures of covered porches.

Jubilee tip: Heaven is in the Sears catalog.

SEPTEMBER 30

New Mexico, 2015, age 55

Our dog Nan is always on duty when she's outside. I feel bad sometimes because she never seems to get a break. She runs the property line and barks across the road to the dogs of the neighboring house. They bark back. Then she begins her rounds again, knowing the neighborhood is somehow safer thanks to her vigilance. Even so, the police force here is so overwhelmed with calls that it's hard to nail the minor offenders. The house next door has had a couple of attempted robberies, so now they have cameras. Another of our neighbors keeps listening to her scanner, and when she gets a good tip, she passes it on to the police. She said the people down the road are dealing drugs and suspected of petty theft. She spent ten years in the police force and walks the streets kind of like Nan but with no barking. She looks like someone's auntie, so she's perfect for the neighborhood watch.

Our Great Dane, Jasper, stands outside, looking in the house window and crying. He is a purebred Blue Merle and one hundred percent baby. However, if there's someone outside that Jasper doesn't recognize, he'll put on his big-boy voice and scare the crap out of them. His size and sound are intimidating, so he puts on a good show. However, Jasper has never met a living soul he didn't want to sniff, lick, and lean on until they sat down so he could prop himself onto their lap. Basically, any intruder on our property would risk being completely loved to death by our dogs. So ... I suppose our neighbor is the real guard dog.

Life seems to revolve around animals. It took me a long time to realize this, and it certainly wasn't something I was taught at a young age. My dad never allowed an animal into our house, so I missed having an inside pet. I see now that together, we have a simpatico existence. The four-leggeds play, and we are entertained. We weep, and they come to comfort us. They bark, and so do we. It's perfect harmony.

Jubilee tip: There's beauty in every beast.

OCTOBER 1

Colorado, 2024, age 64

It has been difficult and tiresome remembering the hard time I had in Connecticut. With the exception of my daughter's death, it was by far the worst time of my life. Trying to communicate the torture I went through ends up sounding monotonous and melodramatic, so I have to stop myself because there are no words that I can write here to tell you just how broken I was.

My children meant everything to me, but I was under a spell. My vulnerabilities were laid bare, and at each turn, this madman Jerry pulled the noose of control tighter around me.

What baffles me now is why my family didn't get me out. I was sick and brainwashed. They knew things were bad enough that they helped take my children from me, but they left me there with this horrible man. I still find this unsettling.

OCTOBER 2

Colorado, 2017, age 57

It's late here, and my dad is dying. He's ninety-seven years old, and he's been in assisted living for a year and a half. Although there isn't really anything wrong with him, he hasn't woken up all day. I wonder if the nurses he punched are glad about it. When his feet started turning blue and his vitals started failing, they called in the family. I wasn't able to make it there in time, so my sister called me on FaceTime. I'm sitting in bed with my wife, Lorraine, watching as he struggles to breathe. It's nearing midnight, and something tells me he's just waiting for it to be my birthday before he goes. I am fighting to avoid taking this moment personally.

It's after midnight now, and my siblings are singing Happy Birthday to me. *Please stop.*

~

He's gone now.

Fuck. My dad died on my birthday, and I watched it on Facetime. **Jubilee tip: Not all things are on purpose (unless your asshole dad dies on your birthday).**

OCTOBER 3

Indiana, 1959, 6:35 a.m. First breath

I had a hard time getting here, and I almost didn't make it, but now I'm here. I am born to Gordon and Iris Given. I weigh nine pounds and eleven ounces, and I'm twenty-one inches long. I have dark, curly hair. The nurses might have thought I was a boy because they wrote "male" on the little certificate they gave to my mother. She fixed it by writing "fe" next to it. I hear her telling my dad about it. I'm holding on. I don't think this time around is going to be easy.

Jubilee tip: You got this.

OCTOBER 4

Indiana, 1972, age 13

Yesterday was my birthday, and my brothers Mark and Jesse got me the best present I have ever gotten. I mean it. Really it is the coolest thing ever besides my bike. I have it on right now, and I'm getting ready to go outside and give it a try. It's sooo neat. It's a complete football uniform. It's red with white stripes, and the jersey is number 13. Yeah, that's right—lucky 13. The football they got me is really great too. My pants have pads, and I just know the shoulder pads will take a really hard hit. The helmet and chin strap fit me perfectly. They even got me socks and some weird underwear with straps—I have no clue how to wear that, so I threw it away.

First thing I'm gonna do is jump into the air as though I'm going for the impossible catch, and then hit the ground hard. This is so crazy cool, and I am so happy. They must really love me.

Jubilee tip: Don't give a girl a jockstrap.

OCTOBER 5

Connecticut, 2003, age 44

"God, do I have to sacrifice myself to be of service and loving to others?"

"Of course not. Who gave you that idea?"

"Jerry."

"What does he know that you don't?"

"He's really smart, God, and I don't know nearly as much as he does."

"What does your heart tell you is true?

"What do you mean?"

"I live in your heart as love, so listening to your heart is when you are closest to Me."

"But what about all the sacrifices I've made for You?"

"I never asked you to do that. Jubilee, when you love others, you love Me; however, when you don't follow your own heart, who are you following?"

(Silence)

"Jubilee, I am your heart. When your heart hurts, I hurt. When your heart is hungry, I'm hungry. To follow Me means to honor your heart, so in aligning with the convictions of your heart, I'll be there."

OCTOBER 6

Vermont, 1985, age 26

These autumn colors amaze me. I love watching Hannah and Molly having so much fun running through the red, orange, yellow, green, and brown leaves. Molly is such a wonder to me. She's tall for her age, and I sometimes forget she's younger than she appears. This makes her a little accident-prone, so I'm keeping a close eye on her.

I love the smell of these beautiful colors, mixed with the distant aroma of burning wood. Granger and I are enjoying some weekend downtime with the girls. We're only here in Vermont for a few days, but we're having such a nice time. I love my family.

OCTOBER 7

Connecticut, 1989, age 30

Hannah and Molly love riding their bikes all around the neighborhood. The Mystic Seaport is just a short distance from our house, so they ride their bikes down by the shore to look across the Thames River. Watching the girls pile up the fallen leaves and then race through them on their bikes makes me laugh. The leaves go flying everywhere as they scream through the harmless crash. Or at least it should be harmless, but inevitably Molly will get hurt. She's so passionate about everything she does, and she's still big for her age. It hurts to see her struggle, but there's no way to hold her back. I try to remind her to go slowly, but she wants to be like her big sister so much that she'll do anything she sees Hannah doing. Hannah is a wonderful big sister, and she definitely looks out for her little sis … they are best friends. Living here in Mystic is good for them. What a beautiful place to raise children.

OCTOBER 8

Kansas, 2020, age 61

Molly's death anniversary seems to begin with my birthday. That year Molly called me on my birthday and sent me an email, as Molly was forever the one who remembered the special dates and bought the gifts and the cards with the money she earned *herself*. Molly would rally everyone to sign my card and be a part of the celebration for each occasion—she *never* forgot. And so I knew she had a present for me that I would get soon. That was Molly. She was a lot more than that, but that was certainly part of who she was.

But that year the gift never came.

On November 16, 1999, I woke up knowing something was wrong. A mother knows when her children are struggling—at least I knew. I felt something was off, so I called my girls. Their stepsister answered, and I asked to speak with Hannah or Molly. Instead, she handed the phone to her mother, my ex-husband's wife, who began erratically spewing her personal drama regarding Molly at me. Granger travels for business often, and this time he was in Kosovo, Serbia. She had once again been left alone with a house full of teenage girls. She was pissed.

"Your daughter is as dumb as dirt, and if you think I will keep her here when she gets herself pregnant, you have another thing coming."

"What's going on?"

Then she spoke incessantly about Molly being grounded from seeing her boyfriend and "violating the terms" and ... blah, blah, blah. Then she told me how she went to Molly's workplace, the Piggly Wiggly, and ridiculed her in front of her coworkers while dragging her out of the store. The whole situation was horrible.

I panicked as I scrambled on the phone to try and pacify her, sympathizing with the difficulty of helping to raise my daughters. Then I did something I would live to regret for the rest of my life ... I betrayed my daughter to maintain peace with Granger's wife.

"I don't want her if she's pregnant," I said. "How will I be able to take care of her? I totally understand where you're at and how frustrating it must be for you ..." I lied.

Even still, the memory of bending over backwards to the devil inside that woman makes my tongue turn into a bitter and deadly thing. How could I ever suggest I didn't want my daughter? Of course, I wanted her—I wanted nothing but her. The separation from my daughters was heartbreaking, but trying to connect with them through the drama of their stepmother seemed impossible.

Then it happened.

I heard it.

The shot fired, and a screaming nightmare ensued.

Holding the phone, in another state, miles, and miles away—I heard the shot, the screams, the horrific narration of my daughter's life draining from her body.

I had to hang up so they could call 911, so I did.

Molly died that night. It must have been around 10:20 p.m. Jerry took the return call and told me she was gone, and I hate him even more for that. It happened on a Tuesday—I hate Tuesdays. There are not enough words to describe the agony of losing a child. There is not enough time or space or screams to express what this horror is like. If I let this grief have its way, it would gut me and leave me for dead; I'm sure of it.

Simone and I left Connecticut to go to South Carolina for Molly's funeral. It was the first time I had seen my siblings in ten years … yes, ten years. They all gathered around me in a Holiday Inn hotel room, where I lay on a bed nearly catatonic. They all placed their hands on me in an attempt to soothe me. They looked into the face of the one they had thought was lost. The prodigal sister.

The next day we held a viewing of her body. Molly was nowhere to be found, and how could that be? She was just here. Where did she go? I mean, how is it that a presence can be here one moment and then gone the next? The idea of seeing her empty body repelled me. I knew if I saw her lying there dead, I would have to accept she was gone. I walked backwards and said no. Then two of my family members took each one of my arms and carried me into the viewing room. I acclimated myself to the room by looking at photographs of her, and then I slowly approached her casket. Molly's hair was the only thing that didn't feel like death, so I touched the beautiful young strands, but she was nowhere around. There was no other choice than to accept she was gone.

At her service, I sang "Amazing Grace." I have no idea how I did that, but I did. Grace has always been a theme in my life, and I sort of hate it. I don't hate grace, but I hate the reasons it is necessary. As much as I don't want to be bitter, I want to challenge All That Is or God or Whoever the Bloody Hell is out there. I want to stand before almighty God and say, "You don't see me at all. You care nothing for my children or me. I don't know why I ever even believed you existed. You gave me a godly mother who tortured and tried to kill me; you gave me a father who beat and molested me. Then you sent Jerry. What has he done but make my life a living hell? They say you gave your only son to die for the sins of humanity, but I don't believe it. I don't believe you have children at all because if you did, you wouldn't let this happen. I don't believe any word from you is true. What the holy fuck, God, could you be any more brutal? I have nothing for you. Nothing."

When the year 2000 rolled around, I told Jerry I was going to my family reunion. Of course, he threatened to open up a can of plague upon my family if I went, but I told him I was going anyway. He accepted it because he had no choice. After Molly died I had more courage and bravery, and I became numb to his threats. At the reunion, I finally saw my mom and dad after eleven years of separation. They weren't well enough to go to Molly's funeral, so the Given reunion was my first time seeing them in all those years.

By 2004, I had left the Jerry cult. Molly's death opened an opportunity ... a window to reunite with my family so I could finally take the steps to find my way out. I don't think she wanted to die. I honestly believe her death was a tragic accident. It just happened to give me a little grace.

OCTOBER 9

New Mexico, 2022, age 63

you come least expected
my smile is your reward
most often accompanied
by my lover's touch
how often I need you
but you
no demands stir you
you cherish the moment of your longing
until
you softly land upon this tortured brow
you kiss with tenderest lips mine
peace
never earned
given
grace

OCTOBER 10 (22)

California, 2003, age 44

Chief Joseph once said, "Good words cannot give me back my children. Good words will not give my people good health and stop them from dying. Good words will not get my people a home, where they can live in peace and take care of themselves.

"I am tired of talk that comes to nothing. It makes my heart sick when I remember all the good words and all the broken promises. There has been too much talking by men who had no right to talk."

OCTOBER 11

Colorado, 2030, age 71

"The way back to yourself is the way to me."
You said that to me nearly ten years ago, and I still love you, Abra.

OCTOBER 12 (23)

New Mexico, 2016, age 57

For the spilled blood of my ancestors, I sit in prayer today. The pages of our history tell a white man's story, but this story is changing little by little. The cries are finally being heard by the Earth's new children. They are being born with new ears. My prayers are for their strength to demand a better way.

Buried atrocities are being exhumed, and the people demand justice. It's happening. Our actions and prayers change the balance of power. The oppressed many join hands instead of leading each other into the jaws of authoritarianism and genocide. Today, I sit in my prayer circle of dirt and rock and give my offerings to the four directions. I release these prayers to ride on the breath of the Earth, to usher in a better way.

OCTOBER 13

Indiana, 1971, age 12

"For our struggle is not against flesh and blood, but against the rulers, against the authorities, against the powers of this dark world and against the spiritual forces of evil in the heavenly realms."

I heard the preacher say these words as he was reading from the Bible. If these enemies aren't flesh and blood, then what are they made of? What devils will I have to fight to get through this life? I'm kinda scared. I know I am pretty strong at sports, but I'm not sure how I'm supposed to fight with invisible things.

OCTOBER 14

Connecticut, 1992, age 33

It has been a year without seeing my girls or talking to them. I asked Jerry again, "Can I please call them? It will be fine—I just need to hear their voices."

He said no.

I ran to the crying rock and sobbed. Then again, I came to him,

"I can't do this. Please understand that I am dying without my children."

He said, "Do you have such little faith in God? Is your small sacrifice greater than the one He made for you? Do you know what treasures await you in heaven?"

My head hung.

"Why don't you make something for them and send it to them?"

I was stunned. "I can do that?" I asked.

"Yes, it is permitted."

"Thank you so much."

I felt so happy and grateful, and I knew just the thing. I am going to make a quilt for each one of my girls. I'll create pictures with fabric and line each one with satin ribbons so they will always be warm and think of me as they fall asleep each night. *Thank you, God, for this precious gift.*

OCTOBER 15

Connecticut, 1994, age 35

I think I died inside my dreams tonight. This is what I remember ...

There is a white corridor with many doors in front of me. I go to each door, open it, and peer inside. There is nothing of particular interest in any of the rooms, so I continue along the passageway. It's sterile, and there is no life here. I want fellowship and to be out among the trees and see the passing of each season, so I keep searching for a way out. I go down some steps. This stairway is cool and damp and dim. I feel my way down. I can hear my heart beating inside my chest, and now, any light from above has faded to black. The air is cold and wet. In this complete darkness, I have only the memory of what I once thought was me.

I am Jubilee.

I try to remember something of my being, but it's useless. This place robs me of all hope and faith, and I fall into a void of memory. I am diminished and estranged. My emotions have shriveled up, and I can make no cry for help. There is no body to warm me. I have given each one of my tears to this dark place. My blood is drained, my breath is vacant, and my vessel is dissolved. I am bereft of even the slightest glimmer of my being. Is there a God?

I've done it. I no longer exist. If there is a God, just do what you will with me. Give me to the dragon as a blood sacrifice if you like. I have no will. I no longer have a life I count as my own. I am finished.

OCTOBER 16

Colorado, 2010, age 51

The West rises within me like a new life. She invigorates my blood and my bones. My skin sheds, and there's a new layer beneath, so I feel new and old at the same time. Snake medicine is coming alive in me. This medicine wriggles and teaches me to embrace the newness of change and to use it for good. The West says she's the record keeper. She remembers all the skins she has shed, and with each new one, she can tell the story of her being. I understand this message. I am the keeper of stories, *the tell* of many. I am living so that others may thrive.

Jubilee tip: Keep track of your skins.

OCTOBER 17

Indiana, 1973, age 14

Today, my dad came into my bedroom to wake me up. He rubbed my back and began caressing my stomach, then his hand went to my private parts. I didn't want him to know I was awake enough to know what he was doing, so I rolled over and tried to deny him access to my body. I feel so sick to my stomach over this, but I can't say anything to anyone. No one can go against my dad without getting hurt. *Why is he doing this to me?*

Jubilee tip: Some people shouldn't be parents.

OCTOBER 18

Kansas, 2020, age 61

My dear, sweet friend is preparing to die. She is a fierce and beautiful soul, and I love her. Her name is Soren Lord, but we have always called her Sulo. Her grand stories are colorful and full of life. Like the times she talked about her personal friendship with William S. Burroughs. He had a cat that he loved, she said, and I guess he shot his second wife. Sounds like he liked his cat more than his wife. Sulo has an unpublished play that Burroughs wrote, and so I suppose her son will have that after she passes.

Sulo went on to tell me of seriously frightening accounts of her father, who was a mortician in Miami, Florida, and used to lock her up in a coffin when she misbehaved. She also said he was personal friends with President Nixon, Billy Graham, and a handful of notable politicians. According to my friend, they were not the good guys we once thought them to be.

Sulo's training was in nursing, and she worked as the director of nursing in San Francisco during the AIDS epidemic. She shared heartbreaking stories about the painful and isolated deaths of so many young men suffering from that deadly virus. These stories have filled me with endless gratitude for her bravery and contribution to this sometimes-hellish existence.

Oh Sulo, my heart longs to be near you once more. I love you, my dear friend.

OCTOBER 19

Kansas, 2020, age 61

Thirty-six years ago a little baby girl was born who would one day start a ripple that may very well heal a world of people. I call people like her keys. They come to open closed doors that are in dire need of unlocking. Sometimes they do it one person, one door at a time, and it's so subtle as to hardly be noticed, but I've watched it, and people are genuinely better having met these ones. Sometimes they challenge the status quo and create obstacles. They come to reveal mysteries and to give others hope and the freedom to live more fulfilled lives. They are anomalies and mysteries even to themselves, but ultimately, they are gifts of growth and light. The one I am referring to is my beloved Abra. Today is her birthday.

OCTOBER 20 (24)

Colorado, 2010, age 51

Today, my friend Arlene and I went to see Grandfather Three Eagles. He's the father-in-law of another friend of mine, and she thought it was time to meet him. He is a Lakota chief, and as my friend tells the story, he died five times at the Sun Dance ceremony and was revived. Like me, he has had many deaths, but unlike me, his were literal body deaths.

Grandfather and his wife live in a modest home in Colorado Springs near the sacred springs where he was born. We got there just before lunchtime. We were instructed that we should take him a gift, so I put together a small box including hummingbird wings, a beautiful stone, sage, and tobacco. He smiled as he accepted our gifts. We enjoyed a lovely lunch together, and Grandfather spoke about his nephew, the Native American singer in the Village People. Seeing his memorabilia collection and hearing the stories he shared was fun.

After our lunch and social visit, we sat together in the living room. Grandfather asked my good friend Arlene and me if there was anything we wanted his help with. I looked at Arlene with an encouraging glance; she spoke to him and asked for his guidance with her life. I listened carefully while trying to muster a question for Grandfather about my life path. After thirty minutes or so, his eyes turned to me.

"Daughter, tell me."

"Grandfather, I am trying to find the questions, but it is all too much. It is too big for me to say any one thing. I can't."

With tears in my eyes, I said, "If you would be so kind as to give me whatever guidance you can about my path …."

He sat silently for a moment and then began to tell me a story.

"When I was a young man, it was my time to do the gourd dance ..."

Grandfather went on to tell me the story of his dance at the Lakota pow-wow and his experience of being entranced in the dance. During the ceremony, Grandfather danced with eagle feathers in one hand and a gourd in the other, shaking them in sync with the drumming. The dance was in full motion. Then one of his feathers fell away from his hand. Time slowed at that moment as the feather began its descent to the ground. His heart sank as the unspeakable unfolded before his eyes. An eagle feather should never touch the ground.

As he stood looking upon the fallen feather, the drumming ceased, and no sound was heard. His uncle came to capture the precious feather. His eagle feather was lost to him, and the dance was over. How could this have happened? The council went into deliberation as he awaited their verdict. There would be no more dancing for him during the remaining days of the gathering. It could have been worse, but the council saw it as a mistake, not intentional neglect.

As he packed his regalia into his trunk, dejected, sorrowful, lacking strength of hope, he stopped and prayed.

"White Buffalo Calf Woman, please help me to understand my path ... give me a sign you are here with me now ...."

Then he told about how a younger man came to him and offered him an eagle feather. It was an act of genuine compassion, and it should have made him feel better, but his heart continued to sink into his chest. As Grandfather began his walk home, there before him on his path lay a white buffalo bone on the ground. Atop the bone was a moccasin with a red stripe down the middle. The red stripe is the good red road, the journey set before us all here on Earth. He knew this was a sign from White Buffalo Calf Woman for him not to lose hope and to know she was always with him on his journey.

As he finished the story, he got up from his soft recliner and disappeared into another room. He returned holding the bone and the moccasin and handed them to me.

"Here, this is your story now, and one day you will give it to another, just as I am giving it to you today."

I am in awe of the gift I have been given. It is among the most cherished gestures I have ever been blessed with. Thank you, Grandfather. I'll continue on my path, knowing I am not alone.

OCTOBER 21

Colorado, 2023, age 64

Abra, Lorraine, and I have decided to live together for a while. It feels right to me, but I'm not sure how long I will last with this arrangement. Lorraine and Abra get along well enough, and that's great, but I still feel that I may need to do something else for part of that time. I can often feel a thing before I can explain what that thing is. Sensing a quietude in my soul that's calling me to sit with it, I know I will follow it. It's my path. I may not leave, but I will follow where my heart leads me.

OCTOBER 22

Kansas, 2020, age 61

I had a dream that I drove off a cliff. It was liberating even though I barely survived. In my waking life, my world swirls so dramatically that this idea of falling over a high precipice is very real to me. My head spins so hard sometimes that I feel like I can barely manage to stay on this planet. Since Dr. Brown stuck the needle into my spinal cord, so much of the time I wonder if I am going to live or die.

Last week, I talked to my sweet young friend who is a long-distance runner. He said he wanted to send me his prize belt buckle from the Hurt 100 Hawaii race that he had just completed. He explained to me that he felt as though he had gone through a kind of death during that race. I asked him to tell me what he meant by that, so he explained what happened to him during the race.

He told me it was pitch dark in the mountain jungle of Hawaii and he was so afraid that he began pleading with God to keep him from stumbling over a cliff to his death. He said the fear of the unknown in the dark had stopped him in his tracks and he couldn't press on until he cried out to God. As I listened to him, I knew we were meant to have this conversation.

His buckle arrived yesterday. I'm so grateful for these timely angels in my life who offer strength, hope, and encouragement to stay the race. I can do this. I'm digging deep and not giving up.

OCTOBER 23

Connecticut, 1990, age 31

I saw Jesus for the second time today. The first time was in a vision, and this time he just came. I have a bad case of strep throat, and it's one of those illnesses my siblings and I get which really clobbers us. So, today I went to see a specialist because I was getting progressively worse. It was after hours, so he was really upset with me. He told me it was irresponsible to wait until after hours to be seen by a doctor and that he had surgery the next morning. I felt terrible, but I didn't know I would be so sick.

He had me sit in the treatment chair in his office as he told me he had to drain the abscess from my tonsil. He gave me a shot to numb my throat, but it didn't work. He didn't care. He dug into my throat while I screamed as loudly as I could. This is when I saw Jesus, right there in front of me, hanging on the cross. The doctor stopped as Granger came racing in because he could hear me screaming from the parking lot. The angry doctor gave me some medicine and sent me home. That's the most pain I have ever felt, and I've had three babies. I'm glad Jesus came to help me out. I kind of think he showed up because he knows what that kind of pain is like.

Jubilee tip: Jesus was a badass.

OCTOBER 24

Kansas, 2020, age 61

A poem.
When things change
I bow to the mercy of the divine
I submit to the wind and lay upon the earth
When tears come, I moisten the soil and breathe into the earth
These woods are dense and lush
Creatures are all around me
When change comes, I may need respite, or I may spring into action
When things change, I may not
I may stand and listen
I may plant my feet and sprout roots
I may lie down and turn to dust
When things change
I may sweep the floors and make the bed
I may sit among friends and laugh
One thing I know for sure
I will never walk away from my one true love

OCTOBER 25

Kansas, 2020, age 61

It has been over forty years since I have been on my own. The last time, I was barely twenty years old. I worked at a Pizza Hut in Illinois and rented a second-story apartment from a nun. She liked me but evicted me as soon as she believed a boy had been spending nights there. It was a guy from Maryland, and we weren't sleeping together. We were just doing massive amounts of cocaine.

Now it's forty years later, and I want the quality of space. There's no need to burn bridges or end relationships. Community and fellowship of an inner circle are as precious as gold to me, and I have no desire to alienate myself from my people. I just want a blank wall to hang my art, a soul mate, my cat, an altar, good food, and a soft bed.

Going deeper, having a lover to share my bed means keeping space with someone who I can breathe with, who can graciously exist with my art, my cat, and my prayers. This I can do.

OCTOBER 26

New Mexico, 2016, age 57

Holy Mother, I see you standing near me now. I know you have come to soothe and heal my wounds. Your healing balm surrounds me, and your divine light fills me. You have sent my daughter, Simone, to me over these thousands of miles to care for me and urge me to wellness. Her presence inspires me to greatness. I am blessed beyond my imagination, and I know you have smiled upon me. I see the aura of your radiance, and with each pulse of light that touches me, my strength returns. My prayers have been heard. I know you love me. Thank you, Holy One, thank you. I have not been forgotten.

Jubilee tip: In all things, be grateful.

OCTOBER 27

Utah, 2020, age 61

I've been driving all day, and I'm so tired. Now in Orem, Utah, I'm sitting up in bed. On the other end of a phone call is my wife. We are not okay. I'm on my way to Oregon to see Abra. Everyone I know seems to be exhausted. My nephew's dog is dying, my daughter's health is compromised, my granddaughter is having seizures again, and I am following a healing path no one else seems to understand. I see it clearly, but it feels like following a scent in the mist on a boat in the dark. With each passing moment, I'm reading signs, having faith in grace, and trusting the way will be made clear. I feel so much depends on me, yet I'm considered crazy.

My daughter thinks I can't make rational decisions for myself and believes I'm irreparably damaged. My inner dialogue is telling me something altogether different. I need to keep following my intuitive guidance, or else what do I have? I've handed my freedom to another before, and I vow never to do it again.

OCTOBER 28

Utah, 2020, age 61

Have the courage to do the unthinkable bewildering things your heart asks of you. Trust like a child who has never been hurt and knows the way will be made clear. I am doing this today, and I hope like hell I can do it again tomorrow.

OCTOBER 29

Connecticut, 1996, age 37

Jerry has been in the payphone business for the past year with three Italian guys who own businesses here in Connecticut and Rhode Island. They have invested in several pay phones, and Jerry runs the business. Jerry is a good salesman and has convinced these guys that the payphone business is a good investment. Weird thing is, the only thing I've seen Jerry do is collect money from these phones and then spend it.

Lately, Jerry has been acting strange. He's been pacing nervously and having private meetings with one of our church members and his wife. I wonder what's going on with him. He has informed me that he's going to admit himself into the Pond House, a secured facility for the mentally disturbed, and that after he's there, he wants me to go and meet with his business associates and plead for his life. He gave me specific instructions. I've never seen him this scared before.

After Jerry admitted himself, I got ready to meet these gentlemen. I put on my prettiest dress and walked down to the little Italian grocery mart. Two portly men were in the back, off the receiving dock. One wore a bloody butcher's apron, and the other was dressed in a gray suit. As I walked up, they turned over vegetable crates to sit on and offered me one. I sat and crossed my legs at the ankle to balance myself.

"Jerry has stolen from us, and he's gotta pay. Our other business partner is so mad he wouldn't even show up for this meeting."

I nodded and said, "I understand how upset you all must be. I can only say that Jerry has had some recent financial emergencies that have caused him to spend some of the profits from the business."

"This is unacceptable, and we ain't gonna let this go."

I pleaded with them, "Please know that Jerry has had a nervous breakdown over this situation and is currently in the Pond House. We are all very worried about him."

"Yeah, you should be worried because, if he doesn't pay this money, he will have more than his mind to worry about."

I lowered my head and took a deep breath. "Jerry isn't a bad man, and he wants to pay you back, but he needs time to replace the money. Can you please agree to a payment plan?"

Both men walked to the door leading back into the business and spoke while I waited.

They returned to say to me, "We want you to know that our business associate who is not here today wants his cut in full, and there is nothing we can do about this, but we have decided to work out a plan with you. We also want you to know that we are not doing this for that rat, Jerry. He's a scumbag, and we don't trust him. The reason we're doing this is because of you. You're a nice lady, and you should lose that guy."

I was incredibly relieved and thanked them for their kindness. As I walked back to the house, all I could think was that I just saved Jerry from being killed by the mob.

Jubilee tip: Sometimes you are the angel.

OCTOBER 30

California, 2008, age 49

My new therapist thinks I'm "mildly schizophrenic." When she said this, I wondered if that was like being mildly pregnant. I mean, either I am or not, right?

As far as I can tell, the psychotherapists of the world are trying their best to keep people from hurting themselves or others. Sometimes I wonder if therapy helps me at all. I've opted out of taking the meds; it just never makes sense for me to take them. Seems to me that medication would make my situation harder to handle. It's just one more thing I can't control. Besides, I can't bear the thought of following in my mother's footsteps. That thought just kills me.

As far as my voices are concerned, they're all pretty nice. I like them, and they like me. I do wonder what constitutes a mild case of schizophrenia though. Maybe it's whispering voices? I get the idea that a mild case is one where the patient (me) decides not to believe every word the voices say … either way, I'm not taking meds.

Jubilee tip: Voices come and go. You decide what's right for you.

OCTOBER 31

Indiana, 1971, age 12

I wish I had someone to trick or treat with me. There's no way I am *not* going out to collect free candy. It started raining, but I don't care. The only problem is that I don't have a costume. But wait … I'll get an old pillowcase and poke holes in it for my eyes. That will keep me dry too. I'll be a ghost. Yeah, that's what I'm going to do.

Jubilee tip: Never give up on free candy.

NOVEMBER 1

Indiana, 1979, age 20

I've been living with my art teacher, Ms. G, these days, but today I went home to visit with Mom. She was lying on the couch, so I asked her how she was doing. She said she was dizzy and felt sick to her stomach. As I looked down at her like so many times before, I felt bad for her. As she was lying there, she looked into my eyes and said, "Would you like me to get up and get you something to eat?" At that moment, I really saw my mother. As ill as she was feeling, she was willing to put aside her own comfort to get me food.

"No, Mom, please just feel better."

I asked her if I could do anything to help her, and she said no.

I feel different now, like all my hurt and pain surrounding my mother turned from black to a lighter shade of gray. I've witnessed my mom's physical and mental health fail all my life, and I have watched her try to make the best of it. Her faith in God has been her storm and her anchor. Her life has been hard, and yet she is a good person in her heart of hearts, and I love her.

Jubilee tip: Good hearts shine through the darkest of times.

NOVEMBER 2

Colorado, 2008, age 49

I want every good thing. I want a love that is true and good. I want to have my cake and eat it too. I want to have enough cake to share with all my friends and then give some to the dogs. I want it all. I want the cake.

Jubilee tip: Eat dessert first.

NOVEMBER 3

California, 1982, age 23

Today, Hannah and I baked bread. She is the most helpful little girl, and I love showing her how to do things. I picked her up and sat her on the counter and then handed her the measuring cup. Hannah held it while I spooned the flour inside and then she dumped it into the bowl. She loves that part. I let her do all the dumping of the ingredients until they are ready to mix, and then I do that part. She loves putting her hands in the dough too. She has the most precious little hands. We really do have so much fun making bread together. Of course, we also get to eat the yummy bread, and when Granger gets home from work, he'll enjoy it too. Being Hannah's mother is the single best thing that has ever happened to me. I love her so much.

NOVEMBER 4

New Mexico, 2010, age 51

My second granddaughter was born today. Sweet little Sonja. Every time I see a newborn baby, I'm amazed that a personality inside a human vessel can just appear. New life is so precious to me. I'll never tire of the mystery of life. Hannah had a difficult delivery … there were complications, and they had to do an emergency C-section. I'm grateful they all got through it safely.

I am so proud of my daughter. I can hardly believe she has four children now. This precious cycle of life marches on, and I consider myself incredibly fortunate to be part of it.

I sometimes wonder if Molly will be reborn as one of my grandchildren. Molly was also born on the fourth, and the number of days between my granddaughters just happens to be the same as between Molly and Hannah. Life is fascinating. Would I recognize Molly if she returned to Earth? I sure hope so. Wouldn't it be great if we had a written manual to understand the ways in which life happens? I love the mystery, but there are some days I really wish I knew more.

Happy birthday, sweet granddaughter; I'm glad you made it safe and sound.

NOVEMBER 5

New Mexico, 2014, age 55

Center place of my circle, I stand before you as my true father. You are the above, the below, and the center of all things. You anchor me to this Earth with the knowledge that I am held in the loving arms of all that is both seen and unseen. You are more than an idea. You are the core of my being, connecting me to the vitality of life.

I stand before you and listen to your words of wisdom.

As you stand before the directions, you have submitted to this life's journey. You continue to trust even though we have tested you. Precious daughter, you are brave to be willing to face your challenges on this Earth. I bear witness to your heart and your walk and ask only one thing of you. My only request is that you never forget how much you are loved. We will always walk with you.

NOVEMBER 6

New Mexico, 2020, age 61

Sulo died this evening, and I swear the planet knows something is different.

Sulo, the force, the storyteller. She is our Lady of Honuback Mountain. She's the reverberating sound from the remover of obstacles. She is the player of the flute, the healer of the downcast, and the shield for the weak.

If you're the would-be purse snatcher, she'll bust you up with her cane and stand over you, challenging you to do better. She is nature herself. I love her, and I always will. *Rest well, dear soul. I know you will always be with us … with all.*

NOVEMBER 7 (25)

Oregon, 2020, age 61

President-elect Biden and Vice President Kamala Harris were announced today. Thank you, God! Abra and I are watching the acceptance speeches together on the couch. It's a historical moment and one I am not likely to forget. VP Harris is the first woman (and woman of color) to be elected to the office of Vice President. It's an incredible step forward for all women in this country. Of course, we need a president who can lead our country with courage and direction—but the stakes seem higher now that we're waging war against this devastating pandemic. We really need someone to step in with integrity to unite the people. I have great hope going forward as I embrace this presidency with faith and gratitude.

NOVEMBER 8

Colorado, 2009, age 50

Lorraine and I are more alike than anyone I have ever met. There's a natural ease in sharing her space. I can talk to her about anything without thinking she may think less of me, and the most important thing I can think of is that I am not afraid of her. For me, this is golden, and there's no way of expressing what this means to me. This safe coexistence is a treasure in my life. I'm not sure what the future holds, yet I'm grateful to have someone like her. If it's only for today, it's enough. If there's more, then fantastic. I consider myself fortunate and smiled upon. That's how I feel about Lorraine. She is my comfort, my safe place, my best friend, and the tether to my kite.

NOVEMBER 9 (26)

New Mexico, 2016, age 57

As far as politics go, I've always kept my distance. There is something about politicians that seems suspicious to me. I've tried to vote for the best-qualified and most genuine person, but I do so with the knowledge that much of what I see is smoke and mirrors. I wish there were a better way to run things. I don't mean to say that I think the government order is a complete failure. Still, I certainly believe there are agendas at work that are not precisely for the people. Today, I watched as our nation ... or really, the electoral college, brought a man into power who I believe has no business leading our country.

I am dismantled and in utter disbelief at what I have witnessed. Donald Trump is going to be the President of the United States. I cannot believe what I'm seeing. I feel as though the entire world is shaking.

NOVEMBER 10

Oregon, 2020, age 61

Whenever I drive by a homeless person, I see a part of me—I recognize desperation and hopelessness. Deep down, I know anyone among us could be one really bad day away from being homeless.

Today, I stopped to talk to a twenty-something-year-old woman holding her sign as her German Shepherd dog lay beside her.

"Hi, how are you doing today?"

"Not so great," she said.

"Is this how you are getting by?"

"Yes."

I handed her a five-dollar bill and went into the Co-op to shop. While I was inside, I bought some flowers for my girlfriend. I passed the young woman again on the way out and saw a glimmer of hope in her eyes. I stopped, put my bag down, and searched for the most beautiful rose in the bouquet.

"For you," I said.

She looked into my eyes and smiled a beautiful smile.

"I hope today is better for you."

I haven't seen her since that day. I hope that means she and her dog are off the street.

Jubilee tip: When you give to another, you give to yourself.

NOVEMBER 11

California, 2057, age 98

Even still at this tender golden age, Creator holds me in Her grace so I can reconcile all of life's colors. If I should lay down my body today, I know the world will not stop spinning or the light and dark of things will not cease to be. Perhaps a few people will show up and say kind things on my behalf, and I will watch and wonder if they, too, understand how the cosmos in all its inexplicable grandiosity exists within themselves.

And as I give my life over to grace, my prayer is that my lover will miss what only she and I shared.

Jubilee tip: Death comes as a lover.

NOVEMBER 12

Connecticut, 1997, age 38

This song is for you, Mother.
(sung to a gentle tune)

When it rains, my hair gets curly
When it snows, my nose gets red
When it's cold, my toes get chilly
When the wind blows, I'm in bed

I say a prayer when autumn leaves fall
I do a jig when music plays
Isn't life so very tempting
When lovely are the changing days

When the trees embrace the roadside
When the snow drifts o'er the plain
Something calls me from the inside
As the day begins to wane

Gentle are the curls that crown me
Flakes of snow land on my head
Warming fires tend to know me
When the wind blows, I'm in bed

NOVEMBER 13

The afterlife

Life's journey seems so simple now. All the things on Earth I thought mattered … not so much. There was never a reason to harm or hate. Fear was nothing but a cloud of deceit. The idea of death is an illusion.

The whole journey was about learning to love. Me as Jubilee was a traveler on a journey to find love for herself and to share with others. Mine was to mirror the light in others back to them.

This was my greatest mission! My smiles are so wide right now because I see it. I see it all, and it really is just that simple. We are love. We are masterful creators, and nothing can separate us from the love that always holds us.

NOVEMBER 14

Oregon, 2020, age 61

There are times when the wind shifts, soul companions appear and hope is lost and then given again. Change seems so cruel at times, and then we see that, after all, change is the most remarkable and caring friend. Change is the best dancer. She loves a good show even when she trips and falls. Change is the wind and the water, and we are the birds and the fish who swim and fly in her currents. Change makes certain the thought of death never comes until, at last, Heaven throws that magical kiss and Mother Earth catches our ashes.

Jubilee tip: Change is synonymous with life.

NOVEMBER 15

Colorado, 2006, age 47

My good friend Arlene came out to the house today, wanting to go out to the listening post. It really is beautiful out there. Our horses, the windmill, the pond, and the wild expanse of land and sky. I walked Arlene out to the post and said she could stay as long as she wanted. I could tell she had something weighing heavily on her mind. I gave her a Sharpie and told her to write the date and her name on the post when she was finished listening. I like keeping track of my listening guests.

As I began to walk back to the house to wait for her, I found matches in my pocket. I walked up to our large heap of rubble that had been piling up for two whole summers. The pile was big. There was old moldy hay, dried-up pallets, and scraps of lumber—but mostly the hay. I'm guessing the pile was a good five feet high and maybe ten feet square, give or take. There was still a bit of snow on the ground, so I thought it was perfectly safe to burn it. So, I lit it.

A small match can start a fire of great force. As the pile took fire, I heard the rush of oxygen suck into the heap. Within thirty seconds that whole thing was ablaze. The horses began to race wildly as the flames grew higher. Whoa! As Arlene walked back from the pasture, she seemed happily astonished. I was flabbergasted as well, and apparently, so were the neighbors. Dee walked out onto the deck, "Honey, is everything okay?"

"Yes, dear, we're just enjoying a fire."

We live on a sixty-three-acre ranch surrounded by other ranches, so it felt safe to assume no one would notice. Wrong.

Soon, off in the distance, red flashing lights approached. Arlene and I wondered if they were coming to our fire, but it seemed unlikely. Wrong again. Regardless, we decided to pull out the water hose and start toning down the flames. The firetruck screamed by and turned onto Ridge Road up on the hill. We didn't think much of it until they turned around and headed directly for us. Before we knew it, they were joining us by the fire.

"Hey! How are you guys doing?"

"Hello there. Ma'am, you can't light fires like this out here."

"Oh wow, I didn't know."

"Right, ma'am. In the future, you need to call the fire department first, and we will give you directions to proceed. Now we need to extinguish this fire."

"Yes, of course."

As they began to work on putting out the flames, they found their hoses were frozen. I offered my garden hose, but they declined.

Indeed, it was a righteous fire, and I was its proud creator. I don't suppose Arlene or I will ever forget it. Holy Smoke.

Jubilee tip: Always keep a garden hose handy.

NOVEMBER 16

Connecticut, 1999, age 40

I woke up this morning knowing something in the world wasn't right. This day has been the single worst day of my life. My Molly is forever gone.

NOVEMBER 17

New Mexico, 2013, age 54

Long shadows fall over me, evening falls over mountain ranges
The east is already dark
The time calls as I watch on in disbelief
Streams lead to the river of my tears
My eyes are swollen with rains of regret
There is no end to it
Oh, my sunshine, how I need you
Knowing you must live on somewhere, how can I rest?
And if you return and knock upon my door
I'll give you my all unless you require less
You'll "ever" know how much I love you*
Please, come then and never take my sunshine away
Molly always made me change this lyric from never to ever

NOVEMBER 18

California, 2004, age 45

November used to be about leaves and the aroma of pies baking
Colors crunched under my feet as someone in the neighborhood lit a fire

I felt safer knowing the cellar was stocked with beets, pickles, and beans

Old man winter was getting cozy by the fire and could barely keep his eyes open long enough to smell the pies

While the old man slept, his clouds and ice appeared

It was a spooky play, and I loved it every year

Then I came into my own summer

It was one summer day in November when winter came too soon

Sleep settled on a spring evening when it was least expected

November said to spring, you are mine

And though the spring could have burst a thousand petals of life into that old cold face

She shuddered in her youth and fell silent

For it was night

We all know that last frost and how some of the early buds are taken

Such was the same in this case

My summer is gone, and autumn is upon me

November's colors are coming back to me now

I can almost smell the pie and the fire

My spring was taken but only for a season

And soon enough, winter will pay me a call

November, you taunted me and filled me

You played outside the lines

Mine was not to be a fresh bud frozen in time

Mine was not the spring to bear it

Mine are the seasons

Come now, November

Fill me once more

NOVEMBER 19

Colorado, 2008, age 49

Every year at this time, I think about Molly and how she left this world. I wonder if her stomachaches as a little girl were a foreshadowing of the shot she fired through her middle. I think about the lessons on gun handling her father gave her and how easy it was for her to locate and operate a loaded gun. There are so many thoughts around that day that never leave me. Did she really mean to die or did she believe she was only going to injure herself? There was that argument with her stepmother, so I know she was very angry. Although I wasn't there, I feel my part in the drama of her life. I wasn't the mother she so desperately needed.

There are some who consider suicide a sin against God, as though it were a one-way ticket straight to hell, but I don't feel this way. My daughter was amazing. To this day, I consider her one of my heroes. She was passionate and brave and would go out of her way to help another person in need. The list goes on and on for just how good I knew she was.

Suicide has a quality about it that makes it different from other deaths. It's sudden and intentional, and of all the other ways one could leave, it feels to me that it would be the easiest one to take personally. As her mother, it is hard to not feel responsible.

NOVEMBER 20

Hawaii, 2004, age 45

I'm in Hawaii with Dee and her son, staying at a cottage on the north shore. The surfing competitions are going on not far from where we're staying; otherwise, there aren't many people around because the surf is so strong. I'm glad to be back on the island again.

The waves are so high they crash upon the shore hard enough to cause a shiver in my spine. I feel compelled to get up in the middle of the night to make sure the waves aren't about to engulf this beach house. Although the waves know the line—tonight, they push to the very edge. There is something in me that doesn't trust a sure thing. I've seen natural things turn in other directions ... like the way a mother is supposed to care for her child and a father, too, for that matter. I'm not afraid; I just don't trust it.

Autumn

NOVEMBER 21
California, 2010, age 51

Sometimes, messages come in sequential waves for me. Last week, it was a dream, and this week, it was the same message but in a different way. Here's what happened:

As I lay dreaming, I heard what sounded as if it could have been the voice of God saying, "YOU ARE A THEOSOPHIST!" The voice repeated this phrase until I awoke. Upon waking, I asked Lorraine if she knew what a theosophist was. We spoke about it for a few minutes, and then I looked it up. The dream left me feeling like I was supposed to get an important message, but I wasn't getting it. I then called my Medicine Woman, and she said that just because someone comes knocking at my door doesn't necessarily mean I need to let them in. I thought about this and thought it must not have been God talking; otherwise, I would have had to take it more seriously.

Then Lorraine and I went on a business trip to Carmel, California; while she met with a client, I visited an old bookshop. The marine layer was thick on the street. The mist in the air gave the shop an eerie vibe, but I liked it and walked in. As I walked around and looked at these old books, one seemed to invite me to reach for it—*The Sacred Doctrine*. Blavatsky. I opened the book and read the exact word I heard in my dream. It's as though that voice wanted to show me something. The author, Helena Petrovna Blavatsky, was the founder of the Theosophical Society. She was a *THEOSOPHIST*. Needless to say, I bought the book, as this was no accident. Maybe the voice I heard was God, and now I need to pay more attention.

NOVEMBER 22 (27)
Indiana, 1963, age 4

It's Friday. The president, John F. Kennedy, died today. He was shot while he was riding in his car with his wife. We have to be quiet and watch the television. Mom and Dad are very sad and crying.

NOVEMBER 23

Colorado, 2010, age 51

Lorraine and I are walking through the woods behind our friend's cabin, and it feels good to be with her here. As I hold her hand, we start climbing a hill and sit together at the top. Her arms are wrapped around me as we look out over the woods below. We're both quietly enjoying the moment when she asks me to marry her. I say yes. She reaches into her pocket and pulls out two beautiful silver necklaces. She places one of them around my neck and then gives me the other one to place around hers. They are matching Celtic wedding knots. I'm pretty sure we just got married.

NOVEMBER 24

Connecticut, 1998, age 39

The pursuit of truth is about getting all the untruths out of the way.

NOVEMBER 25

New Mexico, 2015, age 56

When I left home at the age of 17, I didn't know shit about anything except dodging bullets. My entire world was riddled with lies. Ideas about right and wrong, good and bad, were all tainted and distorted. My perception of life was so messed up that all I knew how to do was survive. I was trying to grasp hold of something that might make me feel acceptable to a displeased God.

My mother was no mother, my father was no father, and God was no good. As grace and my life path would have it, I stayed alive.

Come to find out, after seeking truth for so many years, that there really are very few truths out there to be had. Here's what I have found truth is for me:

Truth is my lover's gaze.

My daughter's smile.

Truth is the friend who brought me dinner a month after my child died.

It's holding my brother-in-law's hand as he lay dying.

Truth is crying and holding my sisters as they tell of the abuse they suffered at the hands of my dad.

Truth is humble and kind. It gives with no thought of judgment. It asks for nothing and gives without regret. It is akin to love and abides with grace.

But most of all, Truth thinks nothing of itself. It just is.

NOVEMBER 26 (28)

Colorado, 2015, age 56

Today, because of our president, Barack Obama, Lorraine and I were legally married—God knows we've already married each other a couple of times in our own ways. This is Lorraine's favorite holiday, and of course, our companionship is something to be thankful for, so we will always celebrate our anniversary on Thanksgiving Day.

However, I have mixed feelings about this day and what it represents. My Native American blood feels as though this day is tainted. I try not to think about the various ways my ancestors were robbed, tortured, and killed … especially on my anniversary, but it's challenging for me. I've decided to celebrate my anniversary as a day of harvest and gratitude, but I will never forget the atrocities of our country and how this land was taken.

NOVEMBER 27

Indiana, 1977, age 18

My art teacher gave me a guitar, and I'm learning to play it. The best thing is sitting on the railing of her deck behind her house and playing for the trees. I love the trees, and there are times when I feel like I can hear them think. They seem to enjoy my playing.

Even though it is a winter day and my fingers are cold, this feels good to me.

NOVEMBER 28

New Mexico, 2009, age 50

We pulled up to 708 Sunset in Williamsburg today, and in front of us was a silver Lexus parked with Honuback Mountain Realty signage on the window. Out walked a rather interesting character with a cane in one hand and a purse on the other arm. I thought of my unruly grandmother for an instant, but this woman smiled such a big smile with no concern at all that half her teeth were missing, so I quickly forgot about Grandma.

Her eyes lit up with a glow that reflected the New Mexico sky, and she belted, "Hello! I am Soren Lord, and I'm so happy to meet you." She kept smiling while making eye contact.

"Hi! This is Lorraine, and I am Jubilee."

"Oh, good! You can call me Sulo."

We followed her up the steps into the sweetest little adobe house we had ever seen. The 18-inch-thick bricks made from the mud of this land help keep the house cool in the desert heat. The door-knobs all had the Zia sun symbol on them, and there was a giant tile Zia sun on the kitchen floor. The kitchen was bright yellow, and there was a royal blue accent wall in the hallway next to the built-in cabinets. The walls curved up to meet the ceiling, and the door-ways were arches. There were no doors except for the bathroom. We fell in love with it. We are going to make an offer. We want to live here, and Sulo is amazing.

NOVEMBER 29

Colorado, 2016, age 57

I've gone to see Dr. Norm Shealy a few times now. He helped me with some lower back issues that were causing me a great deal of pain, so I'm grateful to him for this. The reason I sought him out was because of my near-death event of having a needle inserted into my cervical spinal cord by Dr. Brown. My nervous system is in so much trauma that I feel my life could end at any moment. There are no case studies to see what may happen to me, so he has tried to treat me with some of his existing tools.

Norm has been listed as one of the top ten neurosurgeons and has a long list of innovations including Transcutaneous Electrical Nerve Stimulation (TENS), the RejuvaMatrix® for rejuvenating telomeres, and Transcutaneous Acupuncture, which also rejuvenates telomeres, just to name a few. He tried some of his treatments on me, but one of the side effects of my injury is an extreme sensitivity to electromagnetic frequencies (EMF). When I am exposed to these things, I get sick.

He really did try to help me with his tools and technology, but everything he tried only made me feel worse. Finally, he realized he couldn't help me and then offered to have a confidante meditate upon my condition and send me a reading. I think he is afraid I might die.

The following words are what I received from his friend.

"Stop the negative, self-torturing thoughts from coming into your consciousness. Do not continue to allow them to take over your thought process. They cause you to remain paralyzed in fear: fear of the unknown, fear of making a wrong decision, fear that you have made many wrong decisions in your life, fear of unworthiness, fear of all the confusion you are feeling, fear that no matter what you do, things will not get better for you. These fears and these thoughts need to stop. Immediately. They have taken over your body and mind. They have drained your energy. You feel like you are a robot rather than a person, living life like a machine rather than the way you should. I recommend doing all you can to stop negative thoughts and replace them with fond memories of your accomplishments. Even the smallest accomplishment from your past can make you feel content in the present. Develop a goal list for yourself each day and start working on it. It does not have to be a large achievement, but set a goal for each day for yourself. Then start working on medium-size goals and working toward larger goals. You can do this. You have done this before. This will help you escape the negative thinking you are stuck in."

NOVEMBER 30

Illinois, 1978, age 19

One of the best things I've done so far in college has been making the women's fast-pitch softball team. I'm the first baseman and usually one of the cleanup batters. This past season when we all went down to Florida for the tournament, we went head-to-head with some of the best players I've ever seen. The team that was ranked number one had a pitcher that no one could hit off of. She was just that fast.

It didn't matter I was the clean-up batter since no one else was on base, but I had an idea that if I made myself swing early, I might just have a chance to connect.

It's hard to do a thing that seems unnatural, but I did it anyway, and sure enough, I connected with that impossible pitch and got a double out of it. I was the only one on my team that got a hit off of her.

After the game, she came up to me and shook my hand, congratulating me on getting the hit.

"Not many people can hit my pitches," she said.

I believed her too.

"Thanks," I said.

I felt pretty proud of myself that day.

DECEMBER 1

New Mexico, 2021, age 62

My daughter Simone and I have been through a lot together. This poem I wrote for her. My deepest desire is that she knows just how much I love her.

Defy
So much water
Flows beneath these bridges
Long, sweeping views
Of precipice rock and sky
Graves unmarked
But we know
Where the bones are
And stay clear
Tattooed with invisible ink
Only we see the sign
The other carries
The torrent current
Too dizzy to look down
Between you and I
So high
Any other might die
Greener grasses
Crystal glasses
Rose-colored horizons
Shine and fragrant elixir
Blood in our veins
I'll meet you there
At your shore
Or you mine
Let's defy
And fly

DECEMBER 2

Illinois, 1977, age 18

Yesterday, I think I almost died. The pain I feel is more than I can carry. I swallowed a bag of pills thinking nothing of what might happen other than knowing that something must … happen. I just can't bear my life anymore.

In a state of conscious unconsciousness, I walked over to a hamburger place next to my college campus. I thought I would go someplace and die. I sat down on the bathroom floor next to the toilet; my head was swirling, and my stomach was sick. *Maybe I should buy one of their cheap hamburgers to keep my head from spinning.* I got the hamburger, and then I went outside.

My feet felt as though they didn't belong to my body anymore. There was so much snow on the ground, but I didn't feel the cold.

As I lay down beside the dumpster, I had a vague sense of taking out the trash. I just wanted to sleep. The snow felt soft against my face. Then I closed my eyes.

"Hey. Hey, Jubilee!"

"What?" I stirred.

My brother Doug was there. What was my brother doing there?

"C'mon, let's get you into the car and to the hospital," as he picked me up and put me in the car.

"No, please, don't take me there."

"I have to."

"I feel sick."

He stopped, and I opened the car door. Leaning out and clutching the door's handle, I couldn't stop heaving.

"Please take me back to my dorm room. Please."

"Okay," he said.

We headed back, and I didn't die.

Today, I have an appointment with the college psychologist, and I still can't feel most of my body. I really don't give a fuck what happens now. I just want this horror to stop.

DECEMBER 3

Colorado, 2016, age 57

… again, another reading from the same friend of Dr. Norm Shealy …

"There are those who seem to question and not believe what you have been experiencing. This has been upsetting you and making you feel more and more isolated. You have tried all you can to get help for yourself …. You are not asking for much, just a little improvement in your life. You have been floundering as to what to do. You no longer want to experience pain and want to get back to living your life again. You have struggled in the past, but you now know what needs to change to avoid struggling so much. Your eyes are opening more and more to what has been lacking in your life. Support and comfort were lacking. You have always participated in activities others like, and you've supported and comforted everyone else. You realize now that changes need to occur in your life and want to make them."

I wonder who this person is who seems to know so much about me … how is it that a perfect stranger knows more about me than my friends?

DECEMBER 4

New Mexico, 2015, age 56

Last week Lorraine and I were siding our hay barn and I pinched a nerve in my right shoulder. I usually recover quickly, but this time the pain persisted. There's only one chiropractor in town, so I asked around to see if he was any good. I didn't hear anything bad, so I set up an appointment.

The first appointment was yesterday, and it went okay. Today I felt fine. I felt so much better that I wouldn't have gone back but I owed them money. Yesterday, they would only take a check or cash, and I didn't have either, so I went back today.

This morning my gut kept trying to tell me not to go. God, I should have listened.

One thing about me is that I struggle to see monsters coming. I've had the most challenging time seeing people coming who are going to harm me. I had this conversation with Lorraine just before I left today. Why didn't she stop me? I wish I had listened to the alarms going off inside of me, but I didn't; I just reasoned them away.

I arrived at Dr. Brown's office just as they were closing to go to lunch. He was in a hurry and nothing he did this time was like yesterday. Instead of several small needles, he used one very large needle. He seemed rushed. I told him I felt perfectly fine and didn't think I needed another injection treatment. But he insisted that *he* was a doctor with twenty years of experience and knew what was best for me. I submitted to his authority, thinking I was being paranoid for nothing. He was a doctor after all.

As I lay face down, chin tucked and utterly vulnerable to his negligence, he put a big needle into my neck. That moment changed the course of my life. What I experienced next was an incredibly fierce jolt, accompanied by the intense sound of what I can only describe as a blaring train while simultaneously feeling as though I was being struck by lightning. The intense force threw my left arm to the right and my left leg to the left—both off the treatment table. I was instantly paralyzed on my entire left side. I could not move.

I screamed,

"Please, no! Please don't touch me!" I was at his mercy. "I can't move."

He placed my arm and leg back onto the table. Then he adjusted the table perpendicular to the floor and helped me roll over face up. He continued to adjust my neck manually with hard, calculated movements. I felt my neck crack in his large hands. The pain seared through my paralyzed left side. *Have I been electrocuted?* The moisture in my mouth dried up completely.

"I'm thirsty. I need water."

He went to get me some water.

"Can you please get my phone out of my jacket?"

He got my phone, and with my right hand, I texted Lorraine, "911."

She texted me back, "Are you okay?"

"No."

Lorraine came quickly and helped drag me out of this dark little office.

I'm so scared, but Dr. Brown said I would be fine—just go home and rest … give it forty-eight hours. No emergency room was necessary. Just wait.

He's a doctor, he knows.

As we left, I heard a woman's voice in the waiting room say, "I don't want whatever she had."

I wanted to scream, "Get out!" but it was all I could do to hobble out with Lorraine's help.

Now I'm home on the couch, and I feel as if I might die. I don't know what he did to me, but I'm so sick.

DECEMBER 5

New Mexico, 2016, age 57

A year ago today, I was curled up on the couch hugging my phone looking for answers. That held no other mission than to stay alive. My inner universe was quaking with an undeniable electrical storm. As I lay there in terror, not yet knowing what had happened to me, all I could do was rock, cry, and pray. My whole family was praying, and all I could think about was not dying.

DECEMBER 6

Kansas, 2020, age 61

She has a soul like mine. We're not very much alike, but maybe we were hewn from the same tree. Imagine two vessels being used for different purposes but made of the same wood. It feels like that. The wood speaks to itself regardless of where all its parts reside. Maybe she's the table and I am the chair. It feels completely wonderful, magical, and a little unpredictable. It feels like an answer to prayer for more than just me. She is Abra, and I am Jubilee.

DECEMBER 7

New Mexico, 2015, age 56

I want to live (repeat many times as though counting sheep).
It is not your time to go. Breathe, pray, live.

I'll try and get some rest now.

I want to live, I want to live, I want …

Jubilee tip: Get to the hospital.

DECEMBER 8

Colorado, 2009, age 49

There is an old woman that I see in a mirror when I dream. I've seen her twice now, and it feels like she is me. Her image frightens me, and all I can think is that I don't want her to be me. She's tired and worn out, her eyes are weary, and her back is bent and sore. Her hands are cracked and calloused, and her feet are swollen and aching. She wants to go home. She wants me to see her, and she wants to rest … to go home and be done with dying.

Jubilee tip: Listen to your crone.

DECEMBER 9

New Mexico, 2019, age 60

It has been four years since that dark moment in Dr. Brown's office. I'm feeling better than I did then, but I know I will never be the person I was before that day. I find it very hard to believe this man is still practicing after what he did to me and what I also know he has done to others.

I still remember it so well ….

After having endured the agony of sitting with my injury for a few days, Lorraine got a sitter for me because she had to leave town on business. My internal electrical storm was beyond words. I remember all of it as though it were yesterday.

The incredible pain and numbness began in my left cheek and traveled down my shoulder, down my left arm to my thumb, and then all the way down my left leg and into my toes. It still hurts, but the pain that day was sickening. All l could eat was soup.

But that day with my sitter felt different. I sensed a wall of disorientation approaching my mind. It was like a dense heavy presence of death slowly crossing my head. I knew it was time to finally go to the hospital. This thing might kill me if it got all the way through my head. I had my sitter pack a bag and drive me two hours north to Albuquerque. We let Lorraine know so she doubled back to meet us in Albuquerque.

My sitter and I went to two emergency rooms because no one seemed to know what to do with me. Finally, at Lovelace Women's Hospital, I was able to get the tests done to see what was wrong. I had X-rays and an MRI, and after those results came back, the downtown hospital neurologist wanted me admitted. My sitter and I spent the night in the ER waiting for a bed to become available.

I remember asking my friend if she would hold my feet because they were so cold.

She held my feet, and I fell asleep.

DECEMBER 10

New Mexico, 2015, age 56

My friend sat with me all night. As she held my feet, we talked a lot. I didn't rest very much.

It's morning now, and Lorraine is here with me. Today, they are transporting me by ambulance to the Lovelace downtown hospital, where the neurology department is. It's my first time riding in an ambulance, and I can see the road behind us over my toes. I think about Molly and her ride in the ambulance and wonder if I won't live either.

I've been admitted, and now I'm in my room. I'm in a high-tech bed that rises like a tower behind me, and several machines monitor me. They placed cuffs on both of my legs, and they seem to breathe; the room seems like a giant robot watching everything about me. My nurse is wonderfully gay and colorful, and I feel at ease here, but the staff all look at me with an expression of wonder—I must be different somehow. No one is talking about what might be wrong, but it's as if they know, and they also know that I don't.

My doctor is here now and talking to Lorraine and me. He seems troubled. He pulled a television screen from the wall and is showing us images of my MRI results. He stopped at a picture to enlarge it so we could see it clearly. The image is a circle with a white line going over halfway through it. (The random thought drifts through my mind that the universe is composed of circles and lines.)

"See this?" We're looking, not knowing what we're seeing.

"This is your spinal cord. See this line? This line should not be here. In fact, there is no way this could possibly be here unless everything you've said about what was done to you is true."

What did I say that would indicate a line inside my spinal cord? I'm still not getting it. I look at Lorraine for answers.

"The needle he injected into your neck pierced your spinal cord." The doctor is getting more agitated now. He continued, "I do not know who the hell this guy is, but this is unheard of. He should not be doing this. This is beyond belief and so far beyond the scope of any kind of practice that …" His eyes fell to me mid-sentence, and he said, "I am so sorry."

That's when it really hit me. Dr. Brown had put a needle over halfway into my spinal cord. My lightning-storm raging train that erupted in me has a cause. The doctor is dumbfounded. There is nothing they can do for me, no treatment, and no case study to refer to. They know of no one else that has had this happen to them. How can this be true? I'm the only one?

They assigned me to a stroke doctor, but I didn't have a stroke. Now an occupational therapist is coming to do an assessment. I'll have physical therapy, but they are still observing to see what might happen next. No one knows.

The only other person I can think of who has experienced this kind of accident is Christopher Reeves, Superman, who was thrown from his horse and landed on his head. His cervical spine was severed, and he became quadriplegic.

Now, I feel the kiss of God fully upon my lips. My life has passed through the threshold of death, and yet here I am looking back through that door. No death yet … not even paralyzed. I am spared Mr. Reeve's fate, but how will I know what part of my central nervous system no longer works? Is there a map for such things?

I'm spending the night here and will go home tomorrow. The doctor said caffeine and chocolate would help minimize the bleeding in my spinal cord. *Oh, yay. I get to eat chocolate,* but sadly, nothing more can be done except treat my symptoms going forward. Nothing. There are no other options because the window of time when steroids could have been used to minimize the spinal bleeding has already passed. Dr. Brown had insisted that I wait and do nothing because he was sure my symptoms would pass and he was the doctor.

Dr. M. Brown practices in Las Cruces, New Mexico, and is a menace to society. Heed my warning and do not let him touch you. **Jubilee tip: Doctors should get prosecuted for maliciously manhandling their patients.**

DECEMBER 11

California, 2023, age 64

I'm visiting my brother Jesse in San Diego for a few days. Today, we walked along Ocean Beach together, our feet in the surf.

"Jesse, what was it that caused you to move to San Diego?"

"I've never told you the story?"

"No, I don't think you have."

"It's a long one …."

As we walked along the beach, I listened as he told me the story, citing event after event, synchronicities one after another about how he and his wife and two-year-old son left their life in Illinois and followed the urges of God's direction to San Diego. There were times when he was without a home and a job, scared to death, and yet he continued.

As I was listening to him, I didn't hear any questioning in his voice about his own personal sanity, nor did I hear him hesitate when he was certain of God's direction for him. To the average person, Jesse's actions would have seemed foolish or careless, but as I view his life today and the contributions he has made to his family and his community, his actions brought him to a place of service and fulfillment. Jesse was my childhood best friend … he is my treasured brother, and I've witnessed his journey. He's a good man, but more than these, he has followed his truth, and he is at peace with his inner life.

I couldn't help but relate my own life's events and personal struggles to his story.

Am I compromising what I feel is the right thing to do for the sake of my own comfort and safety?

His story was truly inspiring, but I don't know if I have enough courage to blindly walk out into a hard world at my age. I've already sacrificed so much. After all I have been through, I kinda hate to admit it, but I don't really trust God as much as I used to.

DECEMBER 12

Indiana, 1976, age 17

I'm out on a date with a boy I kinda like. I think he's such a sweet guy. He gave me a pair of black velvet dress pants as a Christmas gift, and I'm not sure I've ever had a present as nice as this before. The snow is coming down pretty hard, but we just pulled into the drive back to my house. He's so polite that he opens the car door for me, and as we stand in the driveway holding each other, we both look up into the night to see the huge flakes of snow falling all around us. It's dark outside, but somehow the snow makes it look as though there is a light on. He kisses me, and I think this is one of the most romantic moments I'll ever know.

Feeling good is such an odd feeling for me, but every year at Christmas time, I get to feel it. I want to thank someone, but I don't know who to say it to. Maybe it's just as well to carry gratitude like a secret in my heart.

Autumn

DECEMBER 13
California, 1981, age 22

Granger's mom is on her way to come and help me with the baby because my due date is today. I'm nearly as big as a barn, but I haven't gone into labor yet. She can only stay for a week, so I hope I'll have my baby while she's here. She's knitting a little sweater set for her. I know it's a girl, and I'm naming her Hannah Michele. I've been getting her crib painted and making a hanging mobile for her made of felt stars of different colors. I'm so excited to be a mother, but I am also a little scared. I want to be a good mom, but I don't know very much about it. I think I can do it. I almost have everything ready.

DECEMBER 14
Colorado, 2001, age 50

Lorraine and I were invited over to Kitty and Arlene's house for dinner last night. Since they're our best friends, I didn't think much about it. However, Lorraine knew I was being set up. After dinner, they said they had a gift for me. I thought that was kind of unusual because it was too early for Christmas presents, but whatever, sometimes they're like that. I went into the living room and had a seat.

Arlene came out with three boxes and a large envelope.

Each box had a number on it so I would know which box to open first. The first box was a pair of Levi's, and on the back pocket, there was a white ring bleached into the denim. Inside the pocket was a can of Skoal chewing tobacco.

Arlene said,

"Jubilee, you're a lesbian so it's time you started acting like one. This is your butch kit."

The next box had a muscle shirt and a red and blue flannel shirt. Not really my style but okay. Then came a smaller box. I opened it up to find a black studded wallet with a long chain attached to it.

According to Kitty and Arlene, my purse-carrying days were over, and now I was expected to carry a wallet. I suppose the chain is for security.

After opening my butch kit, they handed me a contract to sign. The contract stated all the rules of being butch including the preferred footwear—hiking boots being the most logical choice. The terms also forbade me from wearing lipstick. I found this to be particularly unreasonable.

I am now a member of the lesbian butch club.

DECEMBER 15

Minnesota, 1985, age 26

Granger and I are enjoying quiet time together tonight. We just put Hannah and Molly down to bed. Molly always seems to have issues with her stomach—I think it's because she has difficulty quieting her body. What she seems to like the most is when I lay my hand on her belly as she rests her tiny hand on top of mine. Within minutes she drifts off to sleep. Tonight Granger and I are listening to George Winston on the piano while lying on the floor of the living room. We take turns rubbing each other's backs, which is very nice. There is snow outside, but it is warm and cozy here. We have a good life.

DECEMBER 16

Colorado, 2018, age 59

My Medicine Women and I have a bond. We are bound to walk with integrity. We come from a place of peace where there is no competition and no killing. This Earth is not like that. We must remain safe so we can help with the evolution of the human spirit. We are here to do this work.

When they shared this information with me, I had difficulty believing it, but my experiences with near-death encounters have taught me to believe what they have said is true.

I've considered the darkness, and it isn't just the dark—it's the ignorance and malevolence that generate it in the hearts of others that is the foe. It thirsts for diminishing whatever would extinguish it. This darkness is secretive and self-seeking. It longs for material wealth and earthly power over lives. It lives to put out the light … as truth and light are a threat to what lurks in the darkness. My Medicine Women have placed shields around me and have taught me to do the same. If you are here on a similar path, I recommend you protect yourself and keep shining.

DECEMBER 17

Indiana, 1970, age 11

We always get our Christmas tree on Mom's birthday. It's so much fun to get the tree and decorate it while we celebrate. Tonight, we're going to walk up the street to my aunt and uncle's house to cut down a tree; then, Dad will drag it home, and we'll start decorating it after dinner. I hope Mom doesn't mind us doing it on her birthday because I think it makes her big day even more special. The only thing that could make it better would be if it snowed, and I think it might. Happy birthday, Mom!

DECEMBER 18

Indiana, 1975, age 16

The closer it gets to Christmas, the more the Universalist church in town plays Christmas music from the tall bell tower. It's pure magic. The temperature gauge reads thirty degrees, and it's snowing outside now, and the music is playing. I'm going to sit out on the porch and listen—it's like a gift before Christmas. It's the music of the angels in this small town delivered directly to me. I'm going to thank the baby Jesus for this one because it is nearly his birthday.

DECEMBER 19

Heaven, 1959, age not yet

The God talk.

"Jubilee, what do you want on Earth?"

"Do you mean everything I want?"

"Yes, everything. Don't leave anything out that is important to you. All I ask is that you don't give too much attention to what you don't want."

"Okay, this sounds like fun ... you said everything, right?

"Yes, everything."

"On Earth, I see myself being financially independent, with good health, and having a job I love.

"I want to paint, write good books, and sing in such a way that makes others happy.

"Should I keep going?"

"Yes, keep going."

"I would like to live close enough to my family so that I can visit with them often. I would also like to have a cat.

"My lover, hmm, she is perfect for me. She stimulates my mind and my creative urges; she makes me laugh from the soles of my feet, and my cat will love her. She amazes me with her beauty and intelligence. She is always kind and compassionate. She comes to me in our bed and shows me all of her, and I'll know it is safe to show her all of me. She turns me on like no one else. She comforts my heartache. She's clever but not too clever, and most of all, she loves me for who I am."

"You're doing great! Keep going. I want to hear all of it."

"I want to look inside myself and in the mirror, too, and believe I'm beautiful. I would like clear eyes, good skin, sweet breath, and strong hair ... and muscles; I want to be strong.

"In this life, I would like to be accepted, trusted, understood, and forgiven for my failures. I would like the courage to follow my convictions no matter how difficult they may seem.

"I would like to eat good food and have Shakespeare recited to me for a small fee. I would like music enough to dance with my lover, my children, and my grandchildren … all under a beautiful starry night.

"I would like a studio where I can create art with big, glorious windows. I would very much enjoy honest, kind, and critical feedback when I ask for it.

"This sounds like too much?"

"No, not at all."

"Okay then, so I want to be protected but not so much that it keeps me from learning life's most valuable lessons.

"I want dinner parties with great friends, and I want to always trust and think the best of others … and stories, lots of stories.

"I would like my days to be filled with kindness, compassion, thoughtfulness, humor, and grace. I would like to jump and run and then laugh and roll in the grass because of how silly I am. I want to stand in the rain and be nourished. Thunderstorms and magnificent shows of lightning! Please bring me hummingbirds, owls, hawks, and ravens … all to tell me of their adventures … and wishing rocks, lots of wishing rocks, where the sediment lines travel all the way through. I want my dog to lean against me so I can feel the warmth of his love for me."

"Is there more?"

"Are you sure?"

"Yes, please, everything."

"I would like to cry so hard that my face looks like a puddle of flesh, but then it will be one less burden I'm carrying. I want to hold my friends so tight in the hour of their need and not try to fix one thing about them. I want to be able to spot monsters just so I can avoid them or steer an innocent clear of them. This one is really important.

"I want to show every other human I encounter the same love and grace I would like on planet Earth, and finally, I would like to die in the arms of my beloved and walk through the holy veil back to You, knowing I did a good job.

"How was that?"

"That was just fine, Jubilee. I think you're ready."

Jubilee tip: God cares.

DECEMBER 20

Colorado, 2024, age 65

I heard my Creator God speak to me today, flowing through me in a stream of softly spoken words. This Great Divine is my guide, my compass. As I listened, this is what I heard.

"Jubilee, I love you. You are a good-hearted servant. Do you remember now? You came to do a good service. What you knew so well before being born here, you also knew you would have to discover again. The fall to this planet was hard on you. It meant separation from what you loved most. It meant being swallowed by this world of darkness and weeding through the thicket to find the pearl of great price. This act carries with it a very great light, and this light will help others see more clearly. Look into yourself. Go to the tell of Jubilee. It is written inside you, and there you'll remember and see.

"This world and the forces of darkness have tried very hard to kick you off your rails. It has bombarded you with delusional ideas, it has crept up behind you and attacked you in the night … it has frightened you, lied to you, and assaulted you, but you have stood the test of these trials. You have found your way back to you, to Me.

"Believe now that grief is not your natural state. Give yourself permission to be happy and at peace with all life's adventures and challenges. It's time to live in the truth of who you are and why you are here.

"I'll say it again …. In the searching and finding, you not only find yourself but you also find Me in you. For each one on this planet who is doing this great deed, it fuels the light needed for others to see.

"Nothing can stop you or hinder your progress, for you will never be kept from being who and what you are. You are fulfilling your destiny even when you don't think you are … even when you doubt and want to give up. Even when you can't take one more step and then you do.

"You are Jubilee Given, and I am proud to call you Mine."

THE END.

POSTSCRIPT

How does anyone know if her life is a success? As I ponder the answer to this question, I must consider the societal norm for success. Do I have a roof over my head? Am I happy with my work? Do I have plenty to eat? Are my loved ones secure? Am I adding to the health of this planet and those I share it with? These are questions to which we universally want the answer to be yes. These are all important in our daily lives, and we collectively accept them as essential, so we strive for them. There is no denying this.

I was born into a world of circus mirrors. What I was taught was "normal and acceptable" trained me to walk into chaos and pain. What I believed was right and true in my home led me along a path that resulted in terror. I walked through my early years as though I were an innocent deer unknowingly meandering into a goblin's cave. Even in the face of blatant abuse, I could see only the sheep and never the wolf. I was taught no sense of self or personal physical boundaries. What I find inexplicable is the grace I was given.

The years have taught me that I process differently from most people, and I know I'm not alone—maybe you are like this too. I struggle to recognize the ill-meaning individuals in life. Still, I'm grateful for the gifts that help me navigate in precarious situations. I depend heavily on my uncanny intuition, my capability to respond under pressure, and my ability to help others in times of need. Although I've always had an uncanny survivor's intuition, I've struggled at times with believing what it told me.

Ultimately, I believe I am doing my very best, and I'm content and happy on any given day—that seems like success to me. I still grieve the moments in my life that resulted in pain for others. I will forever long for my deceased daughter on this physical plane, but I am confident our paths will cross again. I miss her so much. I know, without a doubt, that my early childhood development left me without strengths that would undoubtedly have helped me in my adult life. Similarly, like Jubilee Given, I can ultimately forgive the broken parts of myself and others and carry on. This, too, is a type of success.

Nothing says we cannot have peace, joy, and love in our lives even amidst the most challenging times. Circumstances come and go. As I look at the wonder of nature with its beautiful displays of expression, I am reminded that life is very much like this. We are all beautiful, natural souls in our cycles of change and growth. Yes, storms and chaotic events test and blindside us, but as the seasons change, there is healing and restoration. I encourage all to approach life this way. Be like the reed that bends in the wind. Be like a tree rooted deeply in the soil. Bow to the seasons and know it's all intentional. You'll know the reasons in due time. Stay intimate with your God through your prayers and petitions. There will be a brighter day. Above all else, believe you are loved and cared for and that grace will escort you into peace and purpose.

To all my fellow travelers, I say, stick to the good red road and fare thee well.

Jia Apple
2024

HISTORICAL NOTES

(1) December 30, 2020, COVID-19 Pandemic

The coronavirus disease 2019 (COVID-19) pandemic is a global outbreak of coronavirus – an infectious disease caused by the severe acute respiratory syndrome coronavirus 2 (SARS-CoV-2). Cases of novel coronavirus (nCoV) were first detected in China in December 2019, with the virus spreading rapidly to other countries across the world. This led WHO to declare a Public Health Emergency of International Concern (PHEIC) on 30 January 2020 and to characterize the outbreak as a pandemic on 11 March 2020. https://www.who.int/europe/emergencies/situations/covid-19

(2) January 6, 2021, 2021 storming of the United States Capitol

The heavily armed, Trump-incited mob attack of Jan. 6, 2021, was an attack not just on the U.S. Capitol building but also on democracy and the rule of law.
https://www.americanoversight.org/investigation/the-january-6-attack-on-the-u-s-capitol

(3) January 16, 2003, Holocaust trains

GERMAN RAILWAYS AND THE HOLOCAUST
https://encyclopedia.ushmm.org/content/en/gallery/german
-railways-and-the-holocaust-photographs

(4) January 28, 1986, Space Shuttle Challenger disaster

On January 28, 1986, NASA and the American people were rocked as tragedy unfolded 73 seconds into the flight of Space Shuttle Challenger's STS-51L mission. Presented below are documents and resources about the accident and its aftermath.
https://www.nasa.gov/challenger-sts-51l-accident/

(5) February 1, 1960, Greensboro Sit-Ins

The Greensboro sit-in was a civil rights protest that started in 1960, when young African American students staged a sit-in at a segregated Woolworths lunch counter in Greensboro, North Carolina, and refused to leave after being denied service. The sit-in movement soon spread to college towns throughout the South. Though many of the protesters were arrested for trespassing, disorderly conduct, or disturbing the peace, their actions made an immediate and lasting impact, forcing Woolworths and other establishments to change their segregationist policies.
https://www.history.com/topics/black-history/the-greensboro-sit-in

(6) February 3, 2016, Heyoka

A Heyoka is a very powerful healer and empath who feels the emotions and energy of others inside their body. The Heyoka is perhaps the most powerful Holy Man or Medicine Man, as s/he has the natural ability to help heal physical afflictions, emotional issues, and or simply bad moods often using humor.
https://www.linkedin.com/pulse/heyoka-shaman-mysticism-4-tom

(7) March 7, 1965, Bloody Sunday

Nearly a century after the Confederacy's guns fell silent, the racial legacies of slavery and Reconstruction continued to reverberate loudly throughout Alabama in 1965.

On March 7, 1965, when then-25-year-old activist John Lewis led over 600 marchers across the Edmund Pettus Bridge in Selma, Alabama, and faced brutal attacks by oncoming state troopers, footage of the violence collectively shocked the nation and galvanized the fight against racial injustice.
https://www.history.com/news/selma-bloody-sunday-attack-civil-rights-movement

(8) April 4, 1968, Assassination of Martin Luther King, Jr.

Shortly after 6 p.m. on April 4, 1968, Dr. Martin Luther King, Jr. was shot and mortally wounded as he stood on the second-floor balcony outside his room at the Lorraine Motel in Memphis, Tenn. He was pronounced dead at 7:05 p.m. at St. Joseph Hospital.
https://www.archives.gov/research/jfk/select-committee-report/part-2a.html#:~:text=Shortly%20after%206%20p.m.%20on,Lorraine%20Motel%20in%20Memphis%2C%20Tenn.

(9) April 18, 1983, 1983 United States embassy bombing in Beirut

1983 United States embassy bombing, a terrorist attack on the U.S. embassy in Beirut, Lebanon, on April 18, 1983, that killed 63 people. The attack was carried out as a suicide car bombing, in which a Chevrolet pickup truck that had been packed with about 2,000 pounds of explosives sped through the gate of the U.S. embassy in West Beirut and struck the building. The resulting blast killed 32 Lebanese workers, 17 Americans, and 14 other individuals. Among the Americans killed were a journalist and eight members of the Central Intelligence Agency (CIA). About 120 others were injured.

Islamic Jihad, a group linked to the Iranian-backed Shīite Muslim militia group Hezbollah, claimed responsibility for the attack. https://www.britannica.com/event/1983-United-States-embassy-bombing

(10) May 19, 2020, Malcolm X

Malcolm Little was born to Louise and Earl Little in Omaha, Nebraska, on May 19, 1925. His father died when he was six years old—the victim, he believed, of a white racist group. Following his father's death, Malcolm recalled, "Some kind of psychological deterioration hit our family circle and began to eat away our pride" (Malcolm X, *Autobiography*, 14). By the end of the 1930s, Malcolm's mother had been institutionalized, and he became a ward of the court to be raised by white guardians in various reform schools and foster homes ....
https://kinginstitute.stanford.edu/malcolm-x Stanford University

(11) May 28, 2020, George Floyd Murder

Four years ago, protests erupted across the country after millions of Americans watched the chilling video of the murder of George Floyd – a Minneapolis police officer, Derek Chauvin, kneeling on his neck for 9 minutes and 29 seconds.
https://www.nbcnews.com/news/nbcblk/george-floyd-death-anniversary-police-reform-rcna153980

(12) July 12, 1976, Barbara Jordan

While the world watched during the Impeachment hearings of President Richard Nixon, Barbara Jordan boldly took center stage. As a lawyer, a congresswoman, and a scholar, Jordan used her public speaking skills to fight for civil and human rights. In 1972, Jordan became the first African American woman to be elected to Congress from the South since 1898.
https://www.womenshistory.org/education-resources/biographies/barbara-jordan

(13) July 16, 1999, John F. Kennedy, Jr., plane crash

John F. Kennedy Jr. died in a tragic plane crash on July 16, 1999, with his wife Carolyn Bessette Kennedy and sister-in-law Lauren Bessette. The son of late President John F. Kennedy and Carolyn, a fashion publicist, were on their way to Rory Kennedy's wedding with Carolyn's sister, Lauren, then a vice president at Morgan Stanley, when the aircraft plunged into the Atlantic. https://people.com/john-f-kennedy-jr-death-what-to-know -7560877

(14) August 9, 1974, Watergate scandal

In the early morning hours of June 17, 1972, a night guard at a D.C. hotel and office complex was making his rounds when he noticed a suspiciously taped-open exit door. He quickly alerted authorities, setting off a series of events that would forever change the nation. https://www.fbi.gov/history/famous-cases/watergate

(15) August 13, 1968, Vietnam War

The Vietnam War pitted communist North Vietnam and the Viet Cong against South Vietnam and the United States. The war ended when U.S. forces withdrew in 1973 and Vietnam unified under Communist control two years later. https://www.history.com/topics/vietnam-war

(16) August 21, 1972, Hanoi Jane

Jane Fonda was photographed seated on a North Vietnamese anti-aircraft gun; the photo outraged American officials and war veterans. When the actor Jane Fonda was arrested in Washington, D.C., on Oct. 11, during a demonstration for action on climate change, it was part of a long history of activism by the actor.

Fonda's activism also made news last year, with the debut of a

documentary about the subject – as well as when then-*Today* host Megyn Kelly called out the actor for an infamous moment in her past, one that has a complicated backstory.
https://time.com/5116479/jane-fonda-hanoi-jane-nickname/

(17) August 23, 1981, Charles Manson

Charles Manson was a cult leader whose followers carried out several notorious murders in the late 1960s, after which he was sentenced to life in prison.
https://www.biography.com/crime/charles-manson

(18) August 28, 1963, I Have a Dream

"I Have a Dream" is a public speech that was delivered by American civil rights activist Martin Luther King, Jr. during the March on Washington for Jobs and Freedom on August 28, 1963, in which he called for civil and economic rights and an end to racism in the United States. Delivered to over 250,000 civil rights supporters from the steps of the Lincoln Memorial in Washington, D.C., the ...
https://www.youtube.com/watch?v=vP4iY1TtS3s

(19) September 11, 2001, September 11 attacks

September 11 attacks, a series of airline hijackings and suicide attacks committed in 2001 by 19 militants associated with the Islamic extremist group al-Qaeda against targets in the United States, were the deadliest terrorist attacks on American soil in U.S. history.
https://www.britannica.com/event/September-11-attacks

(20) September 15, 1963, 16th Street Baptist Church bombing

It was a quiet Sunday morning in Birmingham, Alabama—around 10:24 on September 15, 1963—when a dynamite bomb exploded

in the back stairwell of the downtown Sixteenth Street Baptist Church. The violent blast ripped through the wall, killing four African-American girls on the other side and injuring more than 20 inside the church. It was a clear act of racial hatred: the church was a key civil rights meeting place and had been a frequent target of bomb threats.
https://www.fbi.gov/history/famous-cases/baptist-street-church -bombing

(21) September 21, 1975, Patty Hearst

Around 9 o'clock in the evening on February 4, 1974, there was a knock on the door of apartment #4 at 2603 Benvenue Street in Berkeley, California. In burst a group of men and women with their guns drawn. They grabbed a surprised 19-year-old college student named Patty Hearst, beat up her fiancé, threw her in the trunk of their car, and drove off. Thus began one of the strangest cases in FBI history.
https://www.fbi.gov/history/famous-cases/patty-hearst

(22) October 10, 2016, Chief Joseph

Chief Joseph (1840-1904) by Jim Kershner

"Chief Joseph (1840-1904) was a leader of the Wallowa band of the Nez Perce Tribe who became famous in 1877 for leading his people on an epic flight across the Rocky Mountains. He was born in 1840 and he was called Joseph by Reverend Henry H. Spalding (1803-1874), who had established a mission amongst the Nez Perce in 1836. Young Joseph and his father soon returned to their traditional ways in their Wallowa homeland in Oregon. When Joseph grew up and assumed the chieftanship, he was under increasing governmental pressure to abandon his Wallowa land and join the rest of the Nez Perce on their reservation near Lapwai, Idaho. Joseph refused, saying that he had promised his father he would never leave ..."

(23) October 12, 2016, American Indian Wars

The Indian Wars began the moment English colonists arrived in Jamestown, Virginia, in 1607, when the settlers started an uneasy relationship with the Native Americans (or Indians) who had thrived on the land for thousands of years. At that time, millions of indigenous people had settled across North America in hundreds of different tribes. But between 1622 and the late 19th century, a series of wars and skirmishes known as the Indian Wars took place between American Indians and European settlers, mainly over land control.

(24) October 20, 2010, Gourd Dance

History of a Warrior's Dance—Gourd Dancing

Autumn Whitfield Madrano

The first thing to know about the gourd dance is that unless you're Kiowa, you probably haven't seen it—even if you think you have.

Inspired both by legend and history, the gourd dance ceremony is an essential part of the Kiowa people. Make that the Tdiepeigah, which loosely translates to both skunkberry and brave and is the name used by the Kiowa instead of the generic term gourd dance; the gourd refers to a rattle. Whether you attribute Tdiepeigah to the Kiowa warrior, who was taught the songs by a red wolf who instructed him to teach them to his people, or to the honoring of battles fought by Kiowa warriors during their migration from the northern plains to what is now Oklahoma, both oral history and flesh make it clear this is a warrior dance.

Elements of the gourd dance were originally part of the sun dance, which was banned by the federal government in the late 19th century. Fast-forward to Armistice Day 1946: The gourd dance was revived for the first time in 20 years at a ceremony honoring Indian veterans in Carnegie, Oklahoma. This prompted another revival in 1955 at the American Indian Exposition in Anadarko, Oklahoma. "The sound and sight of this ceremony that had been repressed moved many of the elders to tears," said Dennis Zotigh, a Kiowa Gourd Clan member whose great-grandfather, Harry Hall Zotigh, was one of the revivers of the dance. Thus, the Kiowa Gourd Clan was born.

https://ictnews.org/archive/history-of-a-warriors-dancegourd-dancing

(25) November 7, 2020, Kamala Harris

Kamala D. Harris is the Vice President of the United States. She always fights for the people – from her barrier-breaking time as District Attorney of San Francisco and Attorney General of California to proudly serving as a United States Senator and the Vice President.

https://www.whitehouse.gov/administration/vice-president-harris/

(26) November 9, 2016, Trump claims astounding victory as America's 45th president

BY JULIE PACE AND ROBERT FURLOW WASHINGTON (AP) — Donald Trump claimed his place Wednesday as America's 45th president, an astonishing victory for the celebrity businessman and political novice who capitalized on voters' economic anxieties, took advantage of racial tensions, and overcame a string of sexual assault allegations on his way to the White House.

His triumph over Hillary Clinton, not declared until well after midnight, will end eight years of Democratic dominance of the White House and threatens to undo major achievements of President Barack Obama. Trump has pledged to act quickly to repeat Obama's landmark health care law, revoke America's nuclear agreement with Iran, and rewrite important trade deals with other countries, particularly Mexico and Canada.

As he claimed victory, Trump urged Americans to "come together as one united people" after a deeply divisive campaign. https://apnews.com/article/fb2e92a47f054019a2589ace7 8d20836 The Associated Press 2024

(27) November 22, 1963, Assassination of John F. Kennedy

NOVEMBER 22, 1963: DEATH OF THE PRESIDENT

Shortly after noon on November 22, 1963, President John F. Kennedy was assassinated as he rode in a motorcade through Dealey Plaza in downtown Dallas, Texas.

By the fall of 1963, President John F. Kennedy and his political advisers were preparing for the next presidential campaign. Although he had not formally announced his candidacy, it was clear that President Kennedy was going to run, and he seemed confident about his chances for re-election. https://www.jfklibrary.org/learn/about-jfk/jfk-in-history/november-22-1963-death-of-the-president

(28) November 26, 2015, Obama: Supreme Court Same-Sex Marriage Ruling 'A Victory For America'

June 26, 2015, 11:30 AM ET By Scott Neuman

President Obama called the Supreme Court's decision affirming the constitutional right of same-sex couples to marry a "victory for America" that had "made our union a little more perfect." In the 5-4 decision, Justice Kennedy wrote the opinion of the court, saying the equal protection clause of the 14th Amendment to the Constitution requires states to issue marriage licenses to same-sex couples. "Our nation was founded on a bedrock principle—that we are all created equal," the president said at the White House Rose Garden following the announcement of the decision in Obergefell v. Hodges. Obama said that, often, progress on the journey to equality "comes in small increments. Sometimes two steps forward, one step back."

"And then sometimes there are days like this, when that slow steady effort is rewarded with justice that arrives like a thunderbolt," the president said.

"When all Americans are treated as equal, we are all more free," he added, acknowledging that "Americans of good will continue to hold a wide range of views on this issue."

"For all our differences, we are one people—stronger together than we will ever be alone. That has always been our story," Obama said.

"Today, we can say in no uncertain terms that we made our union a little more perfect."
NPR; https://www.npr.org/sections/thetwo-way/2015/06/26/417731614/obama-supreme-court-ruling-on-gay-marriage-a-victory-for-america